An Introduction to the Nexus 7

D1584858

Jim Gatenby

BERNARD BABANI (publishing) LTD
The Grampians
Shepherds Bush Road
London W6 7NF
England

www.babanibooks.com

C0000 002 659 866

Please Note

Although every care has been taken with the production of this book to ensure that all information is correct at the time of writing and that any projects, designs, modifications and/or programs, etc., contained herewith, operate in a correct and safe manner and also that any components specified are normally available in Great Britain, the Publishers and Author do not accept responsibility in any way for the failure (including fault in design) of any project, design, modification or program to work correctly or to cause damage to any equipment that it may be connected to or used in conjunction with, or in respect of any other damage or injury that may be so caused, nor do the Publishers accept responsibility in any way for the failure to obtain specified components.

Notice is also given that if equipment that is still under warranty is modified in any way or used or connected with home-built equipment then that warranty may be void.

First Published – October 2013

British Library Cataloguing in Publication Data:

A catalogue record for this book is available from the British Library

ISBN 978-0-85934-744-0

Cover Design by Gregor Arthur

Printed and bound in Great Britain for Bernard Babani (publishing) Ltd

Preface

The Google Nexus 7 is a leading example of the new breed of tablet computers; although tiny and very inexpensive, the Nexus 7 is just as powerful as many laptop and desktop computers. The Nexus 7 was introduced in 2012, with a new edition arriving in 2013. A larger version, the Nexus 10, was launched in 2012, the numbers 7 and 10 referring to the diagonal measurement of the screen in inches. The two versions of the Nexus 7 and also the Nexus 10 all use the Android Jelly Bean operating system, so they are used in the same way with a common user interface. **This book was prepared using both versions of the Nexus 7 and most of the material is also applicable to the Nexus 10.**

The first chapter compares the Nexus 7 with other types of computer and outlines its many applications such as news, entertainment, Web browsing, e-mail and social networking. Setting up the Nexus 7 and connecting to the Internet is discussed, followed by the basic methods of operation and alternative input devices and accessories. The Home and All Apps screens are discussed, together with obtaining and installing "apps" from the many thousands available in the Play Store. As are moving, removing and managing apps.

The various Settings are discussed, including Aeroplane Mode, and Screen Rotation, Location Access and features such as Google Cards, Google Now and the Calendar. Browsing the Web using Google Chrome is discussed at length. eBooks, music, video, YouTube and live and catchup TV are described, together with e-mail and social networks such as Facebook and Twitter.

Later chapters discuss "cloud computing" using Google Drive to store files on the Internet, together with the free Google Docs office software. "Syncing" files between computers via the clouds is discussed. Also other methods of transferring files (including photos) between the Nexus 7 and other computers and devices such as SD cards and flash drives. Printing from the Nexus 7 using Google Cloud Print is also explained.

About the Author

Jim Gatenby trained as a Chartered Mechanical Engineer and initially worked at Rolls-Royce Ltd using computers in the analysis of jet engine performance. He obtained a Master of Philosophy degree in Mathematical Education by research at Loughborough University of Technology and taught mathematics and computing in school for many years before becoming a full-time author. His most recent teaching posts included Head of Computer Studies and Information Technology Coordinator. The author has written over forty books in the fields of educational computing and Microsoft Windows, including many of the titles in the highly successful "Older Generation" series from Bernard Babani (publishing) Ltd.

The author has considerable experience of teaching students of all ages and abilities, in school and in adult education. For several years he successfully taught the well-established CLAIT course and also GCSE Computing and Information Technology.

Trademarks

Google, Google Drive, Google Chrome, Gmail, Google Cloud Print and YouTube are trademarks or registered trademarks of Google, Inc. Microsoft Windows, Microsoft Word, Microsoft Publisher, Microsoft Excel and Skype are trademarks or registered trademarks of Microsoft Corporation. Facebook is a registered trade mark of Facebook, Inc. Twitter is a registered trademark of Twitter, Inc. Amazon Kindle is a trademark or registered trademark of Amazon.com, Inc. All other brand and product names used in this book are recognized as trademarks or registered trademarks, of their respective companies.

Acknowledgements

I would like to thank my wife Jill for her support during the preparation of this book and also Michael Babani for making the project possible.

Contents

1

Nexus 7: An Overview   1

The Tablet Revolution   1
The Nexus 7 Really is a Powerful Computer   2
How is this Small Size Possible?   3
Tablet vs Laptop and Desktop Computers   4
Typical Uses of the Nexus 7   5
Keep Your Laptop or Desktop Computer?   6
The Android Operating System   7
The Google Play Store   7
Some Favourite Apps   9

2

Setting Up the Nexus 7   11

Introduction   11
Charging the Battery   11
Starting Up   12
Connecting to Wi-Fi   13
Checking Your Wi-Fi Connection   15
Creating a Gmail Account on the Nexus 7   16
Creating a Gmail Account on a PC or Mac   16
Rotation of the Screen   17
Shutting Down   17
Interacting with the Nexus 7   18
   Touch Screen Gestures   18
   The Menu Icon   18
   The On-Screen Keyboard   19
   The Stylus   19
   Voice Recognition   19

Keyboard Options for the Nexus 7   20
    Connecting a USB Keyboard   20
    Connecting a Keyboard Using a Wireless Dongle 21
    Connecting a Bluetooth Keyboard   22
    Pairing Two Bluetooth Devices   22
Near Field Communication — NFC   23
SD Cards   24
Speech Recognition   24

3

Exploring the Nexus 7

Exploring the Nexus 7   25
The Home Screens   25
The Favorites Tray   26
The All Apps Screen   27
More Apps   28
Customising the Favorites Tray   29
    Removing an App from the Favorites Tray   29
    Moving an App to the Favorites Tray   29
Apps within Folders   30
Customising Your Home Screen   31
    Changing the Wallpaper on Your Home Screen 31
    Deleting Apps from the Home Screen   32
    Adding Apps to Your Home Screen   32
Creating a Home Screen Just for Widgets   33
    A Widget Home Screen   34
    Resizing a Widget   35
Getting Apps and Widgets from the Play Store   35
The Google Play Store   36
Searching the Play Store for Apps   37
    Typing Keywords   37
    Using the Microphone: Speech Recognition   37
Downloading and Installing Apps   38
Managing Your Apps and Widgets   39
Deleting Apps from the All Apps Screen   39
Key Points: Apps and Widgets   40

4

Further Features   41

Introduction   41
Google Now   42
Searching in Google Now   43
    Typing Keywords   43
    Spoken Queries   43
    Sporting Fixtures   44
    Local Information   44
More on Google Cards   45
    Sample Google Cards   46
    Flight Information   46
Settings   47
    Switching the Location Service, GPS and Wi-Fi ON   48
    Quick Settings   48
Notifications   52
My Library   53
The Google Calendar   54
    Creating a New Event   55
    The Calendar Widget   56
    Syncing Your Nexus 7 Calendar with a PC, etc.   56

5

Entertainment   57

Introduction   57
eBooks   58
Google Play Books   58
Reading an eBook   62
Access to eBooks and Other Media Offline   65
Deleting eBooks and Other Media   65
The Kindle App for the Nexus 7   66
Magazines on the Nexus 7   67
    Managing Magazines   67
    Reading a Magazine   68
Music on the Nexus 7   68
Movies on the Nexus 7   70
    Downloading for Offline Viewing – the Pin Icon   70
The YouTube App   71

Live and Catchup Television and Radio 72
Nexus 7 Games 73
Streaming versus Downloading 74
    Streaming 74
    Downloading 74

6

Browsing the Web 75

Introduction 75
Launching Google Chrome 76
Entering the Address of a Web Site 77
The Keyword Search 78
Surfing the Net 79
Previously Visited Pages 80
Tabbed Browsing 81
    Opening a Web Page in Its Own New Tab 81
Using the Google App 82
Bookmarking a Web Page 83
Displaying Your Browsing History 84

7

Communication and Social Networking 85

Introduction 85
Electronic Mail 86
    Creating a Message 87
    Adding an Attachment 88
    Sending an E-mail 88
    Receiving an E-mail 88
Skype 89
    Making a Skype Call 90
    Receiving a Call 90
Facebook 91
    Security and Privacy 92
    Status Updates 92

Twitter   93
    Sending a Tweet   94
    Responding to a Tweet   95
LinkedIn   95
Google+   96

8

Google Drive and Google Docs

Google Drive and Google Docs   97
Google Drive   97
Google Docs   99
    Creating a New Document   99
    Word Processing Using Google Docs   100
    Synchronisation Between Computers   101
Free Word Processing Apps   101
Using the Google Docs Spreadsheet   102
Managing Your Google Docs   103
Transferring Files from a PC to a Nexus 7   105
Cloud Printing from the Nexus 7   107
    Printing a Document Using Google Cloud Print   108

9

Working with Photos and Other Files

Working with Photos and Other Files   109
Introduction   109
Importing Photos from an SD Card   110
Importing Files from a Flash Drive   112
Opening Files from a PC on the Nexus 7   113
Managing the Nexus 7 from a PC Computer   114
Cameras on the Nexus 7   115
Taking Screenshots on the Nexus 7   115
File Security   116
    Viruses   116
    Making Backup Copies   116
    Setting a Password on the Start Up Screen   116

Index

Index   117

Essential Jargon

App

An application or program which a user wishes to run, such as a game, a Web browser or a photo editor.

Operating System

The software used to control the running of a computer, no matter what app is being used at a given time. The Nexus 7 (2013) uses the *Android 4.3 Jelly Bean* operating system.

Processor

A chip which carries out millions of instructions per second to execute an app.

RAM

Random Access Memory. This is the main memory, in which the current app is temporarily stored. The contents of the RAM are lost when the computer is switched off.

Internal Storage

This is permanent storage inside the computer, on which apps and data files can be saved. The Nexus 7 uses an SSD (Solid State Drive) with no moving parts, unlike laptop and desktop computers which use a hard disc drive rotating at high speed.

Cloud Computing

The Nexus 7 saves apps and data files on Google server computers on the Internet, leaving space on the Internal Storage for apps and files which the user wishes to use *offline*.

Offline

Not connected to the Internet. *Offline* would include *aeroplane mode* or computing in places where there is no Wi-Fi access.

Screen Resolution

The number of dots or *pixels* in the screen display. The latest Nexus 7 has a resolution of 1920x1200, or about 300 dots per inch.

Nexus 7: An Overview

The Tablet Revolution

Hand-held tablet computers such as the Nexus 7, Nexus 10 and Apple iPad now meet a lot of the computing needs of many people. The Google Nexus 7 can match the iPad in many respects and is considerably cheaper. Despite its tiny size, the Nexus 7 has real computing power, embracing the latest technology, such as *voice recognition* which really works. Apart from thousands of *apps* for news and entertainment, the Nexus 7 also includes excellent free office software which saves and manages your documents in the "clouds" on the Internet. So later you don't need to worry about where to retrieve them from.

The Nexus 7 Really is a Powerful Computer

As a long-term user of desktop and laptop computers, I was initially sceptical that such a tiny case could contain a powerful computer. In fact, tablets like the Nexus 7 and 10 are more powerful than many of the desktop computers of a few years ago. (7 and 10 refer to the screen's diagonal size in inches). This is confirmed by looking at the critical components which affect the performance of any computer. These are the *processor*, often referred to as the "brains" of the computer and the *memory* or *RAM*, used to temporarily store the app or program currently being used, such as the Chrome Web browser. A *Solid State Drive (SSD)* is used as internal storage where apps and data files such as photos and documents can be permanently saved. The following table compares the original Nexus 7 with the latest version and also the Nexus 10. **Jelly Bean O.S.** refers to the version of the Android Jelly Bean operating system.

	Nexus 7	Nexus 7	Nexus 10
Release date	2012	2013	2012
Jelly Bean O.S.	4.1, 4.2 or 4.3	4.3	4.2 or 4.3
Processor speed	1.2GHz	1.5GHz	1.7GHz
Internal storage	8, 16 or 32GB	16 or 32GB	16 or 32GB
Memory (RAM)	1GB	2GB	2GB
Screen resolution	1280x800	1920x1200	2560x1600
Camera(s)	forward facing (1 only)	forward and backward	forward and backward

Many laptop and desktop computers have inferior processor speeds and less RAM than the latest Nexus 7 and 10. Laptops and desktop computers have more internal storage, typically 500GB or 1TB (terabyte) or more on a *hard disc drive*. The Nexus 7 and 10 don't need this much internal storage, thanks to the use of *cloud computing* discussed on the next page.

How is this Small Size Possible?

How can a powerful computer be fitted into a tiny case like the Nexus 7, when the main base units for some desktop computers are nearly as big as a suitcase? Here are some reasons:

Cloud Computing

The Nexus 7 has no bulky hard disc drive — just a small, compact SSD, as mentioned on the previous page. The Nexus 7 doesn't need a massive hard disc drive because all your documents, etc., are automatically sent to the *clouds*. The clouds are *servers* or computer systems on the Internet with high storage capacity. These include Google's *Drive*, Apple's *iClouds*, Microsoft's *SkyDrive* and *Dropbox* from Dropbox, Inc. You don't need to worry about where your documents are stored or how to retrieve them. You or your friends can access photos or documents etc., stored in the clouds, from anywhere in the world, wherever you can connect to the Internet.

Input and Output Ports

Laptop and desktop computers have lots of bulky ports for connecting monitors, mice, keyboards and printers, etc. The Nexus 7 has only two tiny *ports* or sockets.

The Nexus 7 has a built-in *touchscreen keyboard* which pops up when needed. Tiny speakers, microphones and two cameras are built-in on the latest Nexus 7, so large ports are not needed. The Nexus 7 has a *micro USB* port into which devices such as a keyboard, mouse, SD card or flash drive can be connected. The Nexus 7 is powered by a small battery. The desktop machine requires a *Power Supply Unit* as big as a half a shoebox.

Downloading Music, Video and Software

There is no CD or DVD drive on the Nexus 7, like those fitted to laptop and desktop computers. Early desktop machines also have *floppy disc drives*. Nowadays you can *download* and *stream* music, videos and software (apps) from the Internet to your computer — so you don't need a CD or DVD drive.

Tablet vs Laptop and Desktop Computers

There is currently much debate about whether the tablet will cause the demise of the laptop and desktop computer. It really depends on how you want to use a computer.

I use all three types of computer most days — tablet, laptop and desktop:

- To check the news, weather, look something up on Google, send a short e-mail, listen to music or watch TV I would use the Nexus 7.

- To write a long e-mail, work on a chapter of this book, anywhere in the house, I would prefer to use a laptop.

- To work for a session of several hours using DTP to typeset a book in my home office, I would prefer my desktop machine with its 22-inch screen, large keyboard and mouse, large work surfaces and better ergonomics.

For commuters who need to work on trains or in airports, etc., the Nexus 7 is a good choice, being easier to carry than most laptops and lighter than the 10-inch iPad and Nexus 10.

It has to be said that the Nexus 7 and other mini tablets are a bit small for producing long documents. I find the on-screen keyboard quite tricky to use accurately when typing with the fingers but much better when used with a cheap *stylus*. (Like a pen with a soft tip.)

One solution in the future may be a docking station which converts a tablet, such as a Nexus 7, into the equivalent of a desktop machine, with a separate keyboard, large monitor and a mouse. While away from home or the office, the Nexus 7 is used as a touchscreen tablet. When you return to your base, the tablet is simply plugged into the docking station and used as a desktop machine. In a similar way, I often use a laptop machine connected to a large screen, keyboard, mouse and printer — many of the latest laptop machines are more powerful than desktop machines of a few years ago.

Typical Uses of the Nexus 7

Listed below are some activities for which tablets such as the Nexus 7 are well suited.

- Reading the latest news and weather forecasts.
- Reading online editions of newspapers and magazines.
- Reading electronic books using Google Books or the Kindle app for Nexus 7.
- Listening to music and watching videos.
- Importing and viewing photographs.
- Watching live and catchup TV and radio.
- Searching the Web for information using Google and displaying Web pages using Google Chrome.
- Searching the Web using *spoken* questions.
- Looking at maps, including Google Earth and Google Street View.
- Sending and receiving e-mails.
- Using social networks, such as Facebook and Twitter.
- Buying goods from online retailers such as Amazon.
- Finding out about holidays and booking online, including checking in online.
- Playing games such as Solitaire and Chess.
- Creating and editing text documents and small spreadsheets, including *speech recognition* text input.
- Tracking live flight information of aircraft including location, speeds, altitude, bearing and ETA.
- Managing your online bank account and finances.
- Using the *Skype* Internet telephone service to make free, worldwide, voice and video calls between computers.

Keep Your Laptop or Desktop Computer?

As shown by the examples on the previous page, there's a huge range of activities possible with a tablet computer like the Nexus 7. However, there are some tasks for which you really need a laptop or desktop machine. Fortunately, as the Nexus 7 is relatively inexpensive, currently selling for around £200 depending on the specification, many people may be able to afford a Nexus 7 as well as keeping a laptop or desktop machine.

The following tasks would be easier to accomplish on a desktop or laptop computer rather than on a tablet like the Nexus 7.

- Typing a long document such as a letter, CV, report or student dissertation.
- Desktop publishing, including text and graphics, such as producing and editing a pamphlet, magazine or typesetting a book such as this one.
- Creating and editing a large spreadsheet, balance sheet for a business, personal accounts or large tables of text and figures.
- Design work involving large drawings such as architecture, graphic design, maps or engineering drawings (CAD).
- Creating, editing and updating Web sites.

The main problems with using a tablet for the above tasks are the small screen and keyboard. As mentioned elsewhere, there are various ways to increase the productivity of the Nexus 7. It's also possible to transfer files between a Nexus 7 and a laptop or desktop machine, as discussed later in this book. The laptop or desktop machine may have better software for managing and editing files, although apps are available for the Nexus 7 to carry out many tasks.

The Android Operating System

The *operating system* is a suite of programs or instructions which control every aspect of the computer's running. This differs from *applications* or *apps*, which are programs designed for a specific task, such as reading an e-book, editing a photograph or writing and sending an e-mail. Regardless of what app you are currently running, the operating system is constantly working in the background, controlling such functions as the screen display, saving documents or printing on paper.

The Android operating system for the Nexus 7 is produced by Google and widely used on tablets and smartphones. At the time of writing, in 2013, *Android 4.3 Jelly Bean* is the latest version.

The Google Play Store

Thousands of apps or programs have been developed to work with the Android operating system and these are available from the Google Play Store, either free or costing just a few pounds.

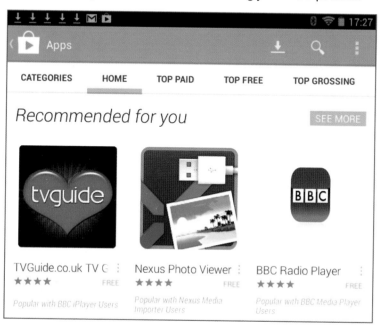

Apps are available for every conceivable purpose from games, music and entertainment, to health, fitness and lifestyle, for example.

Many apps are already installed on the Nexus 7 when you buy it. These appear as icons on the Home Screen, as shown below and on page 9 and 10.

When you install a new app from the Google Play Store, an icon for the app appears on the Home Screen. You can arrange groups of apps in folders representing different categories, such as Music or Photography, for example. The icons can be moved to new positions around the Home Screen. These topics are discussed in detail in Chapter 3.

The Nexus 7 is operated using touchscreen gestures, such as *tapping* and *swiping*. For example, to launch Google, simply use your finger to tap the Google icon on the Home Screen, shown on the next page. Touchscreen gestures are discussed in more detail in Chapter 2. (To launch Google, you can also tap the microphone icon and say the word "Google"). As discussed later in this book, you can also use an inexpensive *stylus*, similar to a pen, or connect a full-size keyboard and mouse.

Some Favourite Apps

The Home Screen displays all the apps installed on the Nexus 7, as shown on page 1. Apps (applications or programs) are launched using a single tap on their icon with a finger or stylus. Listed below are some very popular and useful apps for the Nexus 7, together with their icons.

The **Play Store** icon gives access to thousands of apps in different categories. These are either free or can be bought for a few pounds with a credit card. When a new app is installed on your computer its icon appears on the Home Screen.

Google is the world famous *search engine*. "To Google" means to search for information on a particular subject, after typing in some relevant *keywords.* The Nexus 7 can also use *speech recognition* for entering the keywords.

Google Chrome is a *Web browser*, similar to Microsoft's Internet Explorer and Apple's Safari. A Web browser is used to display Web pages and to move between pages using *links*. You can also revisit Web pages from your *browsing history* or which you have *bookmarked* for future viewing.

Google mail or **Gmail** is a free and popular e-mail service allowing you to send and receive messages consisting of text, pictures and attached files. Creating a Gmail account and password gives you access to several other Google services.

Google Earth allows you to zoom in and view different parts of the globe, using satellite images, aerial photography and images taken by cameras mounted on cars throughout the world. Google **Street View** in **Google Earth** shows 3D panoramic views of houses and buildings, etc., in a locality.

YouTube is a free Google Website which allows individuals and companies to upload and share videos for other people to view. These may include amusing incidents or popular music videos. If a video spreads quickly and is viewed by millions of people, it is said to "go viral".

Skype allows you to make free Internet telephone calls between computers. The Skype app is free and the Nexus 7 has the necessary built-in microphone, speakers and webcams. These enable free *video calls*, as well as voice calls, to be made to friends and family all over the world.

Facebook is the leading *social networking* Web site. Users of Facebook post their *Profile* or *Timeline* on the Internet, allowing them to become online *friends* with people of similar interests. Friends exchange news, information, photographs and videos, etc. Businesses and celebrities can also use Facebook for publicity.

Twitter is another very popular social networking Web site, on which users post short messages or *tweets* (up to 140 characters long). Some celebrities use Twitter to air their views and they may have thousands of followers. You can follow who you like, send replies to *tweets*, or use Twitter to enlist support for a campaign.

The Nexus 7 has its own app, Google Books, for reading e-books, but you can also download the free **Kindle** app, the software used on the Kindle Fire, the original e-book reader from Amazon. There are millions of books, magazines and games available to download cheaply.

Setting Up the Nexus 7

Introduction

When you first take the Nexus 7 out of the box, you may be as surprised as I was that such a slender tablet, (also known as a *slate)*, can house a powerful computer. As discussed in Chapter 1, this is because a tablet doesn't need the bulky components like a hard drive, power supply unit, CD or DVD drive or sockets to accommodate cables for peripheral devices. Thanks to technical advances such as *cloud computing*, based on the Internet, these large components, normally found in laptop and desktop computers, are not needed in tablets.

Charging the Battery

Apart from the Nexus 7 itself, the only other contents in the box are the cable for charging the battery and a couple of flimsy leaflets. No assembly work is needed. Although the battery may be partially charged on delivery, the leaflet advises you to charge it further before you get started. One end of the charging cable plugs into the *micro USB port* on the bottom of the tablet, as shown on the next page. The other end of the cable has a full-size USB connector which can be inserted into a special 3-pin 13 -amp charger, (provided with the Nexus 7). Alternatively the charging cable can be inserted into a USB port on a laptop or desktop computer. Charging via a laptop or desktop computer should be carried out with the Nexus 7 in sleep mode or switched off. This method is slower than when the Nexus 7 is connected to a charger plugged into a 13-amp socket.

Tests have shown that a Nexus 7 with a fully charged battery can be used for 8-10 hours before recharging is needed.

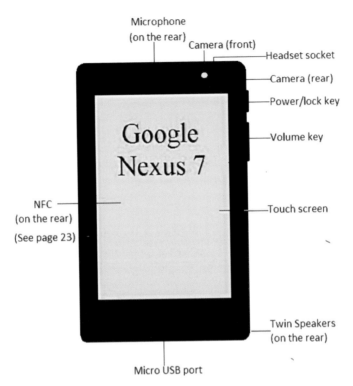

Microphone (on the rear)

Camera (front)

Headset socket

Camera (rear)

Power/lock key

Volume key

Google Nexus 7

NFC
(on the rear)
(See page 23)

Touch screen

Twin Speakers
(on the rear)

Micro USB port

Starting Up

Hold down the **Power/lock** key, shown above on the top right, until the word **Google** appears on the screen, followed by the *lock screen* as shown on the right. *Swipe* the padlock icon by touching it and sliding the finger across the screen. This opens the *Home Screen*, discussed in the next chapter. Normally you'll now be ready to start using the Nexus 7, but with a new computer two more steps will be needed — connecting to Wi-Fi and creating a Gmail account.

Connecting to Wi-Fi

In the home, this often means connecting to a *broadband router*, often included when you take out a contract with an Internet Service Provider such as BT, Virgin or Sky. Or it may mean connecting to the Wi-Fi provided in a hotel or café, etc.

After selecting your language, the Nexus 7 should automatically detect any available Wi-Fi networks. Alternatively swipe down the screen and tap **SETTINGS**. If necessary tap to set **Wi-Fi** as **ON**.

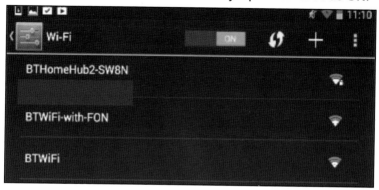

After tapping **Wi-Fi**, you should see a list of available networks.

Tap the name of the router or network which you wish to connect to. The keyboard automatically pops up on the screen, enabling you to enter the password for the network, as shown on the next page. The password can usually be found on the back of a home network router. Otherwise the password should be available from the staff of the establishment providing the Wi-Fi, such as a hotel or café, etc. Tap **Connect** to complete the process of getting online to the Internet. The word **Connected** should now appear next to your selected router or Wi-Fi network, as shown below.

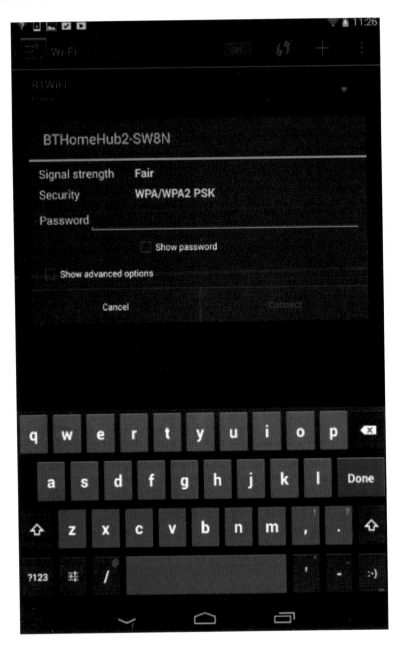

Checking Your Wi-Fi Connection

You can check your Wi-Fi settings at any time by swiping down from the top right-hand corner of the screen and tapping **SETTINGS** as shown in the **Quick Settings** window below.

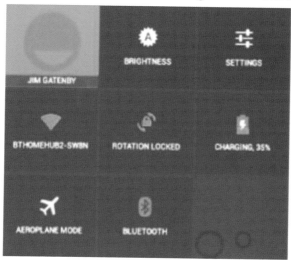

Then tap **Wi-Fi** to display your connection and any other available networks, as shown below

Creating a Gmail Account on the Nexus 7

If you haven't got a Gmail account with an e-mail address and password, you can create one during the initial setting up process for a new Nexus 7 tablet. It's worth opening a Gmail account because it gives access to several other free Google services, such as Google Drive cloud computing, as discussed in Chapter 1, and also Google Docs office software.

You can create a new Google account at any time by swiping down from the top right and selecting **SETTINGS**, as shown on the previous page. Then under **ACCOUNTS**, tap **+Add account**, then tap **Google** and **New**. You are then required to enter your first and last name and choose your e-mail address such as:

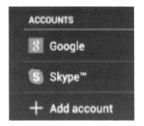

> **jimsmith@gmail.com**

If your chosen name has already been taken you may need to choose a different name or add some numbers, such as :

> **jimsmith77@gmail.com**

Creating a Gmail Account on a PC or Mac

You can also create a new Gmail account using a PC or Mac computer. This will give the PC or Mac access to all of the free Google services such as the *Google Drive* cloud computing and *Google Docs* office software. Log on to **www.google.com** on the PC or Mac and select **SIGN UP**. Then enter your name, your new Google username (ending in @**gmail.com**) and password.

Rotation of the Screen

The screen display can be locked in the vertical or horizontal position, similar to pictures in portrait or landscape mode. Alternatively the screen display can rotate automatically when you turn the tablet between vertical and horizontal positions. To change the rotation setting, swipe down from the top right of the screen to display the

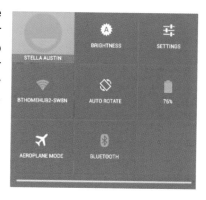

Quick Settings panel, shown above. Then tap the centre button, which acts as a toggle switch between the **AUTO ROTATE** and **ROTATION LOCKED** settings.

Shutting Down

That completes the initial setting up of the Nexus 7 and you should now be ready to start exploring the various screens and apps, as discussed in Chapter 3. As with any computer system, it's always a good idea to follow the recommended shutdown procedure — otherwise work may be lost if files are not closed before shutting down. Hold down the Power/Lock key shown on page 12, until the following window appears. Then tap **Power off** as shown below, followed by tapping **OK** to finish the shut down.

Interacting with the Nexus 7

The next few pages look at the ways we can interact with the Nexus 7 and describe some useful but inexpensive accessories. The methods of operation are:

- Touch screen, the main method of using the Nexus 7, including the on-screen keyboard, using fingers or *stylus*.
- External keyboard and mouse (connecting by Bluetooth, USB cable, or wireless USB dongle).
- Speech recognition.

Touch Screen Gestures

- A single *tap* on an icon opens an app on the screen.
- Tap where you want to enter text and the *on-screen keyboard* pops up ready for you to start typing.
- *Swipe* or *slide* a finger across the screen quickly without hesitating, e.g., to scroll across the Home Screens. Swiping also unlocks a locked screen and opens the Quick Settings window. (Swipe down from the top right).
- *Touch and hold* an item such as an app or a widget, before dragging it to a new position with the finger.
- *Double tap* to zoom in or zoom out of a picture. In some apps *pinching* two fingers together or *stretching* apart can be used to zoom out or zoom in. This is useful, for example, to enlarge a Web Page in Google Chrome or make an area easier to see in the Google Maps app.

The Menu Icon

At the top or bottom right of many screens, the menu icon shown on the right appears. Tap this icon to see a list of options relative to your current activity.

The On-Screen Keyboard

The touch screen method of controlling the computer works very well in most situations. The on-screen keyboard, shown below, pops up whenever you tap in a slot intended for the entry of text.

Hide the on-screen keyboard by tapping the icon shown on the right and on the Navigation Bar above.

The Stylus

If you find accurate typing difficult using the on-screen keyboard, a cheap *stylus*, (under £2) as shown on the right, may help.

Voice Recognition

When entering text in Google Docs, as discussed in Chapter 8, the on-screen keyboard displays a microphone icon, as shown on the centre right. After tapping the

icon, you can enter text, etc., by speaking. The system is remarkably accurate, if you speak fairly slowly and clearly.

Keyboard Options for the Nexus 7

For general use you should find the on-screen keyboard quite adequate. However, for longer documents you might prefer to connect a separate physical keyboard, especially if you type with both hands.

There are 3 basic ways to attach a keyboard to a Nexus 7. (A mouse can also be connected using the same technology.)

- A keyboard connected by USB cables to the micro USB port on the bottom of the Nexus 7, shown on page 12.
- A wireless keyboard connected via a special USB dongle.
- A *Bluetooth* keyboard *paired* with the Bluetooth connectivity on the Nexus 7.

Connecting a USB Keyboard

To use a keyboard which has an integral USB cable, all you need is a small extra USB cable, which converts the Micro USB port on the Nexus 7 to a full-size female USB port, as shown below. These *OTG (On The Go)* cables are available from online retailers such as Amazon, for around £3 or less. Simply plug the micro USB connector into the Nexus 7 and connect the keyboard USB cable to the host end of the small cable. A full-size USB keyboard can be bought for a few pounds.

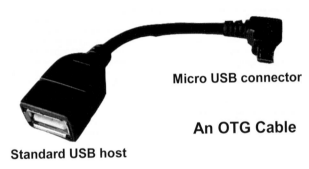

Micro USB connector

An OTG Cable

Standard USB host

Connecting a Keyboard Using a Wireless Dongle

Wireless keyboards (and mice) are cheaply available. These use a *wireless receiver* in the form of a *USB dongle*, as shown on the right. The dongle plugs into the USB host  cable, as shown at the bottom of the previous page. No setting up is required — the keyboard should work straightaway.

Connecting Several USB Devices

A *multi-port USB hub* can be inserted into the USB host cable shown at the bottom of the previous page. This will allow a USB or wireless keyboard, mouse, flash drive and SD card reader, etc., to be connected, simultaneously, if necessary.

Multi-port USB hub

Apps are available to allow files such as photos and documents to be imported to the Nexus 7 from storage media such as SD/ camera cards and flash drives. The *Nexus Media Importer* is available free from the Google Play Store and may be installed as discussed in Chapter 3. This app allows you to import files such as music, videos, photos and documents from a flash drive or SD card.

1. Nexus Media Importer

Connecting a Bluetooth Keyboard

Bluetooth is a type of wireless technology used for connecting devices such as keyboards, mice, headsets and smartphones over short distances. Bluetooth is named after a 10th Century Viking who was credited with uniting Denmark and Norway. Similarly Bluetooth technology connects two electronic devices.

A *Bluetooth keyboard* can act as a *docking station* or *cradle* to support the Nexus 7, as shown in the example below.

Pairing Two Bluetooth Devices

To connect a Bluetooth device, such as a keyboard, to the Nexus 7, the two devices have to be *paired* as follows. On the Nexus 7, swipe down from the top right and from the **Quick Settings** window which appears, as shown on page 15, select **SETTINGS** and make sure **Bluetooth** is **ON**, as shown below.

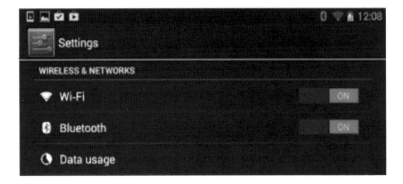

Switch the keyboard on and press the **Connect** button. Tap **Bluetooth** on the Nexus 7, as shown on the previous page. Then tap **SEARCH FOR DEVICES** and the Nexus 7 should detect the Bluetooth keyboard as shown below. When the keyboard is detected you are asked to type a *PIN* or code in using the Bluetooth keyboard.

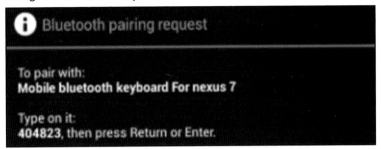

This should complete the pairing process and the Bluetooth keyboard will then be ready to use.

Near Field Communication — NFC

This is a form of wireless communication between two devices in close proximity. The NFC area of the Nexus 7 is at the back of the tablet. Swipe down from the top right of the screen and tap **SETTINGS**, then **More...** under **WIRELESS & NETWORKS**. Make sure **NFC** is ticked and **Ready to transmit app content via NFC** is displayed under **Android Beam**, as shown below.

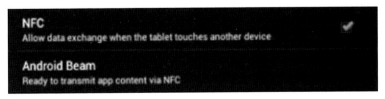

If you place the Nexus 7 back-to-back with another NFC-ready device such as a tablet or mobile phone, you should see the prompt, **Touch to Beam**. Touch the screen to send files such as Web pages and YouTube videos between the two devices.

SD Cards

SD cards are used to record photos in digital cameras. They can also be used to supplement the internal storage on the Nexus 7, which may be 16, or 32GB. SD cards are available in similar sizes up to 64GB. Unlike some computers, the Nexus 7 doesn't have a built-in card reader. However, an *SD card reader*, costing a few pounds, can be connected to the micro USB port on the Nexus 7, using an OTG cable, as shown below and on page 20. Free apps are available to manage the importing of photos and other files, such as documents, as discussed later.

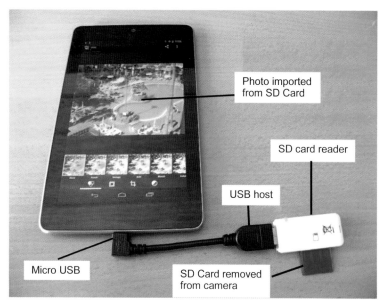

Photo imported from SD Card

SD card reader

USB host

Micro USB

SD Card removed from camera

Speech Recognition

This is a stunning piece of advanced technology. Instead of typing words into a search program such as Google, simply tap the microphone icon, as shown on the right, and speak. For example, try saying **Charles Dickens**. The Nexus 7 responds with a spoken answer and a list of links to relevant Web pages.

Exploring the Nexus 7

The Home Screens

When you first start up the Nexus 7 after holding down the Power key, the first screen you see is the *Home Screen*, as shown on the right. In fact there are five panels on the Home Screen which you can investigate by sliding or swiping horizontally in either direction. The Home Screen is the starting point for your sessions on the Nexus 7, from where you launch *apps* and *widgets*. The latter are small windows which display information such as a calendar, a clock, the weather or a list of your e-mails.

A lot of apps are already installed by default on a new Nexus 7 and you can add more from the Play Store. Icons for your favourite apps can be placed on a personal Home Screen, making it easy to find and open the apps you use the most.

The Navigation bar at the bottom of every Home Screen is shown below. The left-hand icon opens the previous screen. The middle icon opens the central Home Screen. The right-hand icon displays thumbnail images of recently opened apps.

The Favorites Tray

Along the bottom of all the Home Screens is the *Favorites* tray shown below, giving quick access to frequently-used apps. The default apps can be replaced by apps of your own choice.

The icons on the Favorites tray above are as follows:

 This icon launches the **Google Chrome** Web browser.

 Tap to watch popular **YouTube** online videos.

 Google Maps allows you to search for places worldwide and zoom in or out using finger gestures.

 This icon displays the **All Apps** screen shown on the next page.

 Google Mail is an extremely popular e-mail service, discussed in more detail later in this book.

 This opens the **Hangouts** feature where you can send messages to your friends or start a video call.

 This launches the second camera for taking general photographs. (Not fitted to the earlier Nexus 7).

The All Apps Screen

When you tap the All Apps icon on the Favorites tray, shown on the right, the screen shown below appears, displaying up to 30 apps. As discussed later in this chapter, you can find more new apps in the Play Store and install them. Tap **WIDGETS** shown near the top left below to display the installed widgets. Frequently-used apps and widgets can be copied from the All Apps and Widgets screens to locations on the Home Screens, as discussed shortly.

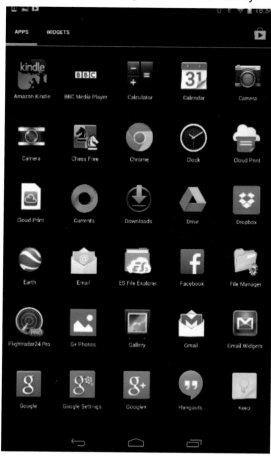

More Apps

From the All Apps screen, slide or swipe to the left to display a second apps screen. When you install new apps from the Play Store, their icons appear on this additional All Apps screen. As mentioned previously, you can move apps around, delete some of them and insert new ones, as discussed shortly.

As shown above and on the All Apps screen on the previous page, there may be a lot of apps on your Nexus 7, some of which you rarely use. You can tailor the Favorites tray to include your most frequently used apps, as described on the next page.

Customising the Favorites Tray

The default Favorites tray on the new Nexus 7 is shown below. The All Apps icon shown on the right and below is fixed on the Favorites tray and cannot be moved or deleted. The other six icons on the Favorites tray represent apps or folders and can be moved or deleted and replaced with apps which you use most frequently.

Removing an App from the Favorites Tray

Touch and hold the icon for the app you want to remove from the Favorites tray. Hold your finger on the icon until **X Remove** appears at the top of the screen. Without lifting your finger, drag the icon over **X Remove** and drop it, deleting the app or folder. Please note that removing an app from the Favorites tray doesn't uninstall the app from the Nexus 7. Its icon still appears on the All Apps screen. Alternatively, move an app from the Favorites bar and slide it onto another part of the Home Screen.

Moving an App to the Favorites Tray

Clear a space on the Favorites tray by moving or removing an icon, as described above. To move an app on the Home Screen to the Favorites tray, hold your finger over the icon, then drag the icon to the space on the Favorites tray. In the example below, the green **Hangouts** icon shown above has been removed and replaced by the icon for the Play Store. The **Maps** app (third from the left above) has been replaced by a *folder* which includes the **Facebook** app. Folders are discussed on the next page.

Apps within Folders

The circular icon shown on the right represents a *folder*, containing several apps. Folders can be created on the Home Screens and on the Favorites bar. For example, you might want to create a folder

for all your games or all your music apps. Or you could put the apps for **Facebook**, **Twitter** and **Skype**, shown below on the Home Screen, in a folder called **Social**, for example.

Touch and drag the icons, one on top of the other, to form a single circular folder icon shown on the left below. Tap the folder icon to reveal the contents and to give a name to the folder if you wish. As shown below, tap **Unnamed Folder** and enter a name of your choice, **Social** in this example. Tap a circular folder icon to view and launch the individual apps within, as shown below.

Customising Your Home Screen

When you start using a new Nexus 7, the default setup may not be to your liking. In fact there are five panels making up the Home Screen. These may already have default apps and widgets which you don't particularly want. You can tailor your Home Screens in the following ways .

- Change the background colour or wallpaper.
- Delete any apps and widgets you don't want.
- Copy from the All Apps screen apps that you want to use regularly and place them on your Home Screen.

This will make a personal Home Screen, showing just your most frequently-used apps and widgets, in addition to those on the Favorites tray. To organise your apps further, you can group them in folders, as discussed on the previous page. Folders can be added to the Home Screens and to the Favourites tray.

(The apps placed on the Home Screens are only *copies*, so removing them from the Home Screens doesn't remove them from the All Apps screen or uninstall them completely.)

Changing the Wallpaper on Your Home Screens

Hold your finger on an empty part of the Home Screen until the following window appears. Tap any of the icons to view the available choices. **Gallery** displays your own photos, **Live Wallpaper** presents moving objects and **Wallpaper** includes various patterns such as the background shown on page 30. Tap **Wallpaper** shown to the right and then tap **Set wallpaper** to apply the new background.

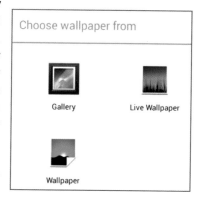

Deleting Apps from the Home Screen

You may have apps on the Home Screen which you no longer use. Or you may think the default Home Screens on a new Nexus 7 are unnecessarily cluttered. You can safely remove apps and widgets from the Home Screens. Tap and hold the unwanted app until **X Remove** appears at the top of the screen. Then drag the app over **X Remove**. As the apps (and widgets) on the Home Screen are only *copies*, they are still available in the All Apps screen.

Unlike the Home Screen, care should be taken with the All Apps screen, where it is possible to *uninstall* apps completely. If the uninstalled apps are needed in the future, they will need to be reinstalled from the *Play Store*, as discussed shortly.

Adding Apps to Your Home Screen

To make up a personal Home Screen with the apps you find most useful, open the Home Screen where you want the apps to appear. Clear the screen of any apps and widgets you don't want. This is done by touching and holding the app or widget, then dragging onto **X Remove**, as described previously.

Tap the All Apps icon as shown on the right then touch and hold the app you want to move to the Home Screen. The Home Screen opens. Keeping your finger on the app, slide it into the required position on the Home Screen. Part of a personal Home Screen is shown below.

Many of the apps on the previous page were obtained from the Google Play Store, discussed later in this chapter. These include the **BBC Media Player** and **BBC iPlayer** (in a folder called **BBC**) and also **Flightradar 24** and **Smart Voice Recorder**.

Creating a Home Screen Just for Widgets

You can launch apps by tapping their icon on the All Apps screen or by tapping a copy of the app you have placed on a Home Screen, as discussed in the previous section. If you tap an icon for a widget in the **WIDGETS** section of the All Apps screen, you are told to **Touch & hold to pick up a widget**. This is because you need to place a copy of the widget on a Home Screen before you can use it.

Although you can mix apps and widgets on the same Home Screen, widgets tend to be much larger than apps and soon fill up the available space on the screen. So you may wish to put your most useful widgets on a separate Home Screen panel.

Clear a Home Screen panel by touching and holding any unwanted apps or widgets and dragging them onto **X Remove**, as described previously. Now open the **WIDGETS** section of the All Apps screen, as shown below, and touch and hold the required widget. Then slide the widget into the required position on the Home Screen.

A Widget Home Screen

The Home Screen below contains widgets for a calendar, news and e-mail. This screen was created as discussed on the previous page by sliding each widget from the **WIDGETS** section of the All Apps screen to a cleared panel on the Home Screen.

Quickly flick the **Current** news widget shown on the top right above to bring successive pages from the newspapers to the top of the stack. Then tap a page you're interested in to display the full article, as shown below, swiping sideways if necessary.

Resizing a Widget

Some widgets can be made bigger or smaller. Hold the widget for a few seconds and release your finger. If a rectangular frame appears with solid blue circles on each side, as shown below, you can drag the circles to resize the widget.

Getting Apps and Widgets from the Play Store

The previous pages described the way you can create your own Home Screens by sliding Apps and Widgets from the All Apps screen. A brand new Nexus 7 has quite a lot of apps and widgets already installed by default on the All Apps screen, including the WIDGETS section.
However, there are many more apps which can easily be downloaded from the Play Store. Many of these apps are free or can be purchased for a few pounds. To open the Play Store, tap its icon shown on the right, on the All Apps screen or on your Home Screen.

The Google Play Store

The Play Store has thousands of apps and widgets and various categories such as games, movies (to rent or buy), music, books and magazines, as shown below.

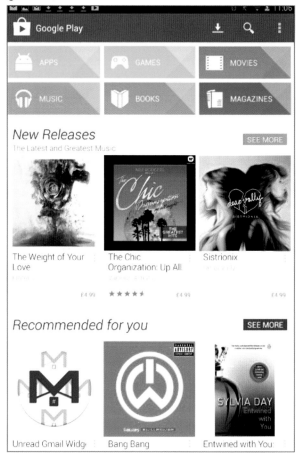

You can scroll through the various categories to find a particular item. Alternatively, you can carry out a search for an item such as an app, game, movie or book, etc., as discussed on the next page.

Searching the Play Store for Apps

As an example, a search will be made for an app for an on-screen music keyboard for the Nexus 7.

First tap **APPS**, as shown on the main Play Store screen shown on the previous page. Then tap the magnifying glass search icon, as shown on the right.

Typing Keywords

The search bar appears as shown below, with a flashing cursor ready for you to type the name of the app or widget you wish to search for. The onscreen keyboard pops up automatically. Enter the keywords for the search, such as **music keyboard** and tap the search key (magnifying glass icon) on the keyboard.

Using the Microphone: Speech Recognition

Tap the microphone icon shown on the right. The small window shown below appears, requiring you to speak the keywords, such as **music keyboard**.

The speech recognition system on the Nexus 7 is most impressive and immediately finds lots of music keyboard apps, as shown on the next page. You might like to practise searching for a few apps using the microphone. Apps I found in this way included **chess game**, **route planner** and **sound recorder**.

Downloading and Installing Apps

The search for music keyboards results in a long list of apps, as shown in the sample below. Most of these are free or at most cost only a few pounds.

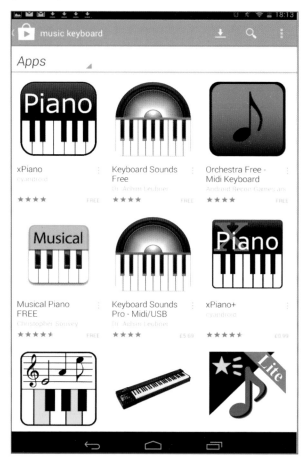

To obtain an app, first tap its icon as shown above. If it's free of charge, the word **INSTALL** appears on the right. If there is a charge, the price is shown on the right, instead of **INSTALL**.

For a free app, tap **INSTALL** to download the app to your Nexus 7. An icon for the app is placed on your All Apps screen and on your Home Screen. The app should now be ready to open and use. If there is a charge for an app, tap the price and you will then need to buy it by providing your bank details, before proceeding to install it.

Managing Your Apps and Widgets

Previous pages have shown how the new Nexus 7 already has quite a lot of apps and widgets already installed by default on the All Apps screen. Some of these can be copied onto a Home Screen tailored to your own requirements. The last few pages showed how you can obtain new apps and widgets from the Google Play Store and install them on your All Apps screen and on your Home Screen(s).

Deleting Apps from the All Apps Screen

Care is needed if you try to delete apps or widgets from the All Apps screen, including the **WIDGETS** section. After touching and holding an app you previously installed, the word **Uninstall** appears at the top of the screen, next to a dustbin icon. If you slide the app over the dustbin icon or **Uninstall**, the app will be removed from the Nexus 7. If you need the app again you will need to reinstall it from the Play Store.

Default Apps or widgets are those already installed on the All Apps screens when the Nexus 7 was purchased. These default apps and widgets do not have the **Uninstall** option when you touch and hold their icons in the All Apps screen.

Key Points: Apps and Widgets

- The Nexus 7 is "driven" by tapping icons representing apps and widgets.

- Apps are small applications or programs such as a Web browser, a game or a drawing program.

- Widgets are small windows, usually displaying information such as a calendar, news or an e-mail inbox.

- The All Apps screen has APPS and WIDGETS sections showing all of the apps and widgets installed.

- The Home Screen consists of 5 panels which can be customized to display selected apps and widgets.

- Apps and widgets are copied from the All Apps screen by touching and holding, then sliding onto the Home Screen.

- Further apps and widgets can be downloaded from the Google Play Store. New apps and widgets are placed on the All Apps screen and the Home Screen automatically.

- At the bottom of every Home Screen is a Favorites tray which displays 6 icons for frequently used apps.

- The user can change the apps on the Favorites tray.

- The Favorites tray also displays the All Apps icon.

- Widgets cannot be placed on the Favorites tray.

- Related apps can be grouped together and placed in folders, such as Painting, Photography, Games, etc.

- Folder icons are circular, can have a name and can be placed on the Favorites tray.

- Apps on the Home Screen are only copies. Deleting them doesn't remove them from the All Apps screen.

- The Navigation bar at the bottom of the Home Screen has icons to return you to the centre Home Screen and to display previously visited screens and app thumbnails.

Further Features

Introduction

Previous chapters have looked at the setting up of the Nexus 7 and the apps and widgets which are the cornerstone of everything you do on this incredibly versatile and powerful device. This chapter looks at some more of the features built into the Nexus 7 and, more precisely, its Android Jelly Bean operating system. The features described in this chapter are:

Google Now and Google Cards

This feature provides Google searching for information using both voice and text queries. Google Cards automatically displays useful, real-time information for your current location.

Settings

Used to switch important settings on and off, make adjustments and tailor the Nexus 7 to your own requirements.

Notifications

This screen keeps you up-to-date with new e-mail messages, calendar events, new downloads, Bluetooth, Wi-Fi, battery strength and aeroplane mode, as discussed shortly.

My Library

This is a widget that displays all the books, movies, music, etc., that are already on your Nexus 7.

Calendar

Keeps track of all your appointments and sends reminders of imminent events, synchronised to your various devices.

Google Now

This is an extension to the popular Google search engine. Google Now employs GPS (Global Positioning System) satellite technology to pinpoint your exact, current location. This is used to gather local information such as the weather and traffic conditions.

Google Now doesn't require any setting up. You just need to make sure **Google Now** is switched on in the **Settings**, together with **Location access**, **GPS satellites** and **Wi-Fi**, as discussed on page 47 and 48.

To open Google Now, swipe up from the bottom of the screen, or tap the Google icon on the Home Screen, shown on the right. The Google Now screen opens with a search bar across the top, as shown below.

In the centre of the screen above is a *Google Card*. This is a small panel which pops up, unsolicited, to show current local information. Google Cards are discussed shortly.

Searching in Google Now

Typing Keywords

The search bar in Google Now shown below allows you to enter the keywords for a search, such as **weather in Florence**, by typing using the on-screen keyboard.

Spoken Queries

You can also tap the microphone icon, as shown above and on the right. Then speak your query into the Nexus 7. Using spoken queries is discussed in more detail on page 37. The results of the search may produce a spoken answer, as well as a Google Card, as shown above. You will also see some traditional Google results as shown below, which you can tap to open Web pages relevant to your search.

Weather in Florence, Italy | 14 day weather outlook of Florence
www.worldweatheronline.com/**Florence-weather**/Toscana/IT.aspx

Latest **weather in Florence** Weather, Italy. Florence 14 day weather forecast, historical weather, weather map and Florence holiday weather forecast.

Weather Map - Florence, Italy weather - Monthly Averages

Perhaps you could experiment with a few spoken queries. For example, I spoke the question, "what is a bantam?" (being a keeper of a few of the little birds). I received the spoken answer, "A chicken of a small breed of which the cock is noted for its aggressiveness." This also appeared on a Google Card together with a list of traditional Google search results, as shown below.

Sporting Fixtures

If you enter or speak the name of a favourite sports team, such as Chelsea FC or Manchester United, Google Now produces a list of their forthcoming fixtures.

Local Information

Similarly you could ask for a forecast of tomorrow's weather, traffic conditions on a particular route or a list of restaurants in your area or in your current location (if using Wi-Fi on the move).

More on Google Cards

Google Cards pop up on the Google Now screen without you taking any action. For example, suppose you enquire about flights at your local airport, or about traffic on local roads. Google Now responds with Google Cards based on your recent activity.

As shown above, Google Cards report on the volume of traffic on the relevant roads and may give a time and a link to a suggested route to a destination, such as an airport. If you tap an information icon, as shown on the right and above, a black panel appears at the bottom of the card. This explains why the Google Card has been displayed.

You've recently searched for Birmingham Airport, Birmingham, Birmingham, B26 3QJ

Sample Google Cards

At the bottom of the Google Now screen, you often see the message, **Show sample cards**. Tap this message to see a list of topics for which Google Cards are available, together with examples. As you can see from the list of sample cards below, Google Cards are available on a wide range of subjects, such as **Weather**, **Traffic**, **Public transport**, etc.

Flight Information

I recently made a Google enquiry about a flight from Frankfurt to Birmingham. Shortly afterwards on the same day a Google Card popped up with the latest flight information, as shown below.

Settings

In order to use Google Now, a number of features need to be switched on. These are probably already switched on by default, but you can easily check, as shown below. The main settings needed to fully use Google Now are:

- Google Now **ON**
- Location access **ON**
- GPS satellites **ON**
- Wi-Fi & mobile location **ON**

If **Google Now** is not **ON**, when you swipe up from the bottom, or tap the **Google** icon on the Home Screen, you only see the basic Google screen, not the more colourful **Google Now** screen, as shown on page 42. To turn **Google Now ON**, tap the menu icon shown on the right and below, at the bottom of the Google screen. (You may need to swipe up to see it).

Show more cards...

From the menu which appears, tap **Settings** and then make sure **Google Now** is **ON**, by tapping **OFF,** if necessary, and then tapping *Yes, I'm in*.

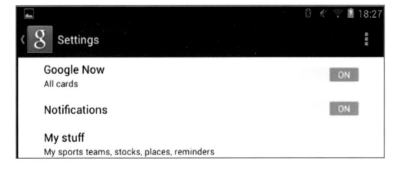

Switching the Location Service, GPS and Wi-Fi ON

Swipe down from the top right of the screen, to display the Quick Settings panel. Then select **SETTINGS** and under **PERSONAL** tap **Location access**. The three settings to enable Google Now to pinpoint your current location are shown below and should be **ON** or ticked. Tap anywhere in a row to change a setting.

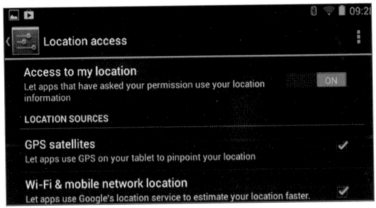

Quick Settings

This feature is available from Android 4.2 onwards and gives direct access to some important settings. Swipe down from the top right of the screen, to display Quick Settings, as shown below.

As can be seen on the Quick Settings panel at the bottom of the previous page, there is an icon to change the brightness of the screen. Tapping **BTHOMEHUB2-SW8N** (in this example), allows you to check your Wi-Fi connection, as discussed in Chapter 2. The icon on the right displays the state of the Nexus 7 battery.

AUTO ROTATE allows the screen to remain upright and readable even when the Nexus 7 is turned on its side through 90 degrees, so that its long edge is horizontal. The alternative setting, **ROTATION LOCKED**, keeps the screen display in a fixed position relative to the sides of the Nexus 7.

BLUETOOTH, shown on the Quick Settings panel at the bottom of the previous page, allows you to detect any nearby devices which have the Bluetooth wireless technology switched on. This includes Bluetooth keyboards and smartphones, for example. A Bluetooth device can then be connected to the Nexus 7 for the exchange of data, etc. This was discussed on page 22.

AEROPLANE MODE, also referred to as **FLIGHT MODE**, switches off signals from the Nexus 7 which might interfere with an aircraft's instruments. When flying, it's advisable to check with the airline before using AEROPLANE MODE, as airlines vary in their rules for allowing devices such as tablets to be used. In AEROPLANE MODE, you can't use the Internet so you won't be able to read ebooks, etc., which are only stored in the clouds. If you want to read ebooks, listen to music or play games during a flight, make sure they are saved on the Internal storage of the Nexus 7 before boarding the plane. This is done by selecting **Keep on device**, as discussed in Chapter 5.

The **SETTINGS** icon shown on the right and at the bottom of the previous page, opens the full screen of settings, as shown on the next page.

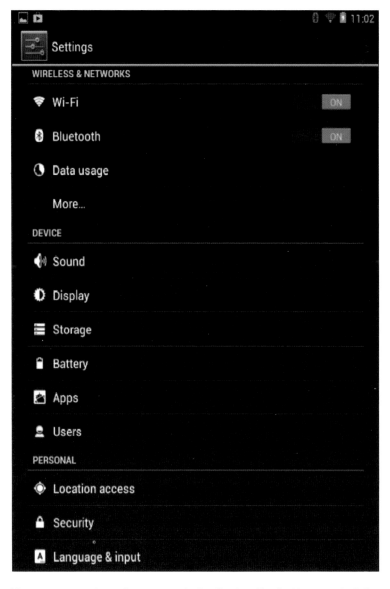

It's necessary to swipe upwards to display the bottom part of the SETTINGS menu, as shown on the next page.

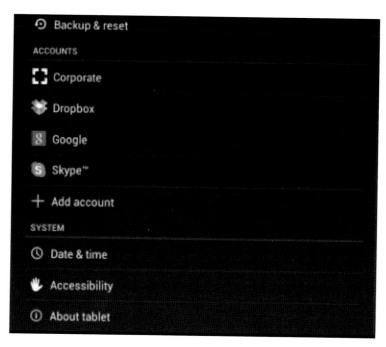

The Settings menu allows you to check your Wi-Fi and any Bluetooth connections. You can alter the screen brightness and wallpaper and the sounds emitted when various events occur. **Apps** on the previous page lists all your applications and gives you the chance to disable them. **Users** lists the people who can use the machine and allows the addition of profile information.

Location access is where you can set up GPS, so that you can access local information. **Security** has many options including the setting of a password required to start using the Nexus 7. You can also limit the installing of apps to those from the Google Play Store and disallow apps from other sources. Play Store apps have been thoroughly checked for malicious software.

Other settings include the creation of accounts on Skype, Dropbox and Google, etc. **Accessibility** provides help for those with special needs such as poor eyesight, etc.

Notifications

Across the top of the Home and All Apps screens you should see two groups of very small icons.

The group on the left above represent events such as receiving an e-mail, capturing a screenshot or events from your calendar (discussed shortly). The group of small icons on the right above are *system icons*. The icons in this group change according to your settings. For example, icons may be present which show Bluetooth ON, sound OFF, aeroplane mode ON, Wi-Fi ON, the battery state of charge and the current time.

To display your notifications, as shown in the example below, swipe down from the top left of the screen. If a notification refers to an e-mail, tap to read the message. Once you've looked at a notification, it's removed from the list.

Tapping the icon, shown on the right and at the top right below, dismisses all notifications.

My Library

This is a widget that displays all the music, magazines, books, and movies that are installed on a Nexus 7. Some of these media may be already installed from new or you may have added more from the Google Play Store.

The **My Library** widget may already be displayed on one of your Home Screens. If not, tap the All Apps icon shown on the right and then select **WIDGETS** at the top. Swipe to the left until you see the **Play – My Library** widget as shown on the right. Touch and hold this widget, then slide into a convenient place on the Home Screen. Tap the title **MY LIBRARY** to display icons for all of your installed media, **My music**, **My books**, and **My magazines**, etc. Tap a thumbnail, e.g. of a book cover as shown in **My Library** on the bottom right, to read the book, listen to music or watch a movie, for example.

Play - My Library   6 x 4

To make room for **My Library**, widgets and apps no longer needed can be deleted by holding and sliding over **X Remove** at the top of the screen. (Removing an app or widget from the Home Screen doesn't totally remove it — it will still be present on either the APPS or WIDGETS screen).

The Google Calendar

The Calendar on the Nexus 7 has many useful features including the following:

- Keeping a record of all your future events.
- Sending you notifications of imminent events.
- Synchronizing changes between various devices, such as your Nexus 7, smartphone, laptop or desktop PC or Mac.

The Calendar on the Nexus 7 can be opened by tapping its icon on the All Apps screen, as shown on the right. There is also an icon for the calendar in the Google+ folder on the Favorites tray on the Home Screens.

The Calendar opens as shown in the example on the right, displaying the events for the current week. An arrow at the top, next to **Week**, opens a menu enabling you to display **Day**, **Week**, **Month** or an **Agenda** listing all of your events. When a **Day** or a **Week** are displayed, the current month is also displayed at the bottom left, as shown on the right. You can scroll through displays of the days or weeks by swiping horizontally. To scroll through a display of the months, swipe vertically.

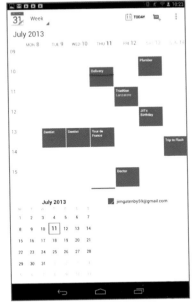

Creating a New Event

Tap the icon at the top of the calendar or tap twice in the correct hourly slot on the appropriate day. The **New Event** screen appears as shown below. Here you can enter the name of the event and the location, time and the names of any guests.

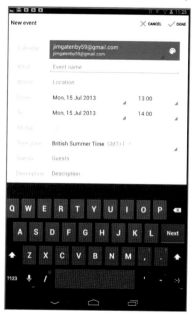

At the bottom of the **New event screen** shown above, (visible when the keyboard is not displayed), you can set a **Reminder** in the form of a notification or an e-mail. With a notification there is a beep and then an event, such as **Barbecue** in this example, appears in the **Notifications** panel, as discussed on page 52. Tap the event name for further details, as shown below.

The Calendar Widget

A Calendar widget appears in the WIDGETS section of the All Apps screen and this can be placed on a suitable clear space on the Home Screen. This is done by touching and holding the widget and then sliding into position on the Home Screen, as described in more detail on page 33. The Calendar widget lists all your forthcoming events, automatically updated with information from the Calendar app. Tap the Calendar widget to open the Calendar app for editing existing entries or adding new events.

Syncing Your Nexus 7 Calendar with a PC, etc.

The Google Calendar can be viewed on all the common platforms — Nexus 7, iPad, laptop or desktop PC or Mac, etc. Just open **www.google.co.uk**. If necessary **Sign in** with your Gmail address (or **Sign up** for a new one). Then select the **Apps** icon on the top right of the screen, shown here on the right. From the drop-down window which appears, select the **Calendar** icon, shown below, to open the Calendar.

New events can be added to the Calendar on any of your devices. Any changes to the Calendar are automatically synced across to all the devices you sign in to.

5

Entertainment

Introduction

Amongst many other things, the Nexus 7 is a versatile entertainment platform. The following activities are discussed in this chapter:

- eBooks — electronic books which may be downloaded from the Internet for reading offline at any time.

- Music, magazines, movies and games downloaded for free or bought or rented.

- YouTube — a Google-owned Web site enabling you to play free music and videos uploaded by other people.

- Live and catchup TV and radio.

The small size and light weight of the Nexus 7 mean you can use it literally anywhere — on a sofa, in bed or in a public place such as a restaurant. You can stow it in a bag and take it on holiday; many places such as hotels and restaurants now have free Wi-Fi so while you're away you can still go online for all your favourite Internet activities. The Nexus 7 may also be used for your personal in-flight entertainment, if your airline allows it. *Aeroplane mode* or *flight mode* must be switched on to prevent possible interference with the aircraft's instruments and potentially serious consequences. This was discussed on page 49 and only allows you to use the NEXUS 7 *offline*, i.e. not connected to the Internet. Such offline activities would include reading an e-Book or watching movies which have been saved for offline use, before boarding the aircraft.

eBooks

Many 20th century projects involved devices for reading books electronically on a screen. The Amazon Kindle, introduced in 2007, quickly became a best-seller, being extremely light and affordable and an efficient alternative to the printed book. Millions of eBooks are available to be downloaded from the Amazon Kindle Store and saved on a tablet such as the Kindle Fire, the iPad or the Nexus 7. A tablet like the Kindle or the Nexus 7 can store far more books than most people are ever likely to read. (Figures in the thousands have been quoted, depending on what you take as the average size of an eBook).

- The Nexus 7 has its own app, Play Books, for reading eBooks and you can use it to download books from the Google Play Store, which contains millions of titles.
- You can also install the free Kindle App on the Nexus 7 and obtain books from the Amazon Kindle Store.

You can always delete any eBooks you no longer want, to save space on the Internal storage of the Nexus 7.

Google Play Books

When you first start to use the Nexus 7, there is already an icon for the Play Books app on the All Apps screen. If you read a lot of eBooks you may wish to copy the icon to the Favorites tray as shown below. The earlier Nexus 7 (Android 4.2 Jelly Bean) had the eBooks icon installed on the Favorites tray by default, as shown below.

Tap the Play Books app shown at the bottom of the previous page. On a brand new Nexus 7, you'll probably find a few books are already installed, as shown below in **My Library**.

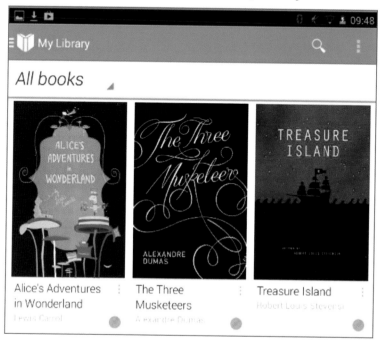

Tap **Read now** or **My Library** (whichever is shown on the top left of the screen) to display the menu shown on the right, which includes the **Shop** option. Tap **Shop** to open the Play Store as shown on the next page.

The Play Store can also be opened by tapping its shopping bag icon shown on the right below and on the right of the Favorites tray on the previous page.

In the Play Store you can browse through the various categories listed down the left, as shown below, check new arrivals and best selling books or look at the top free books.

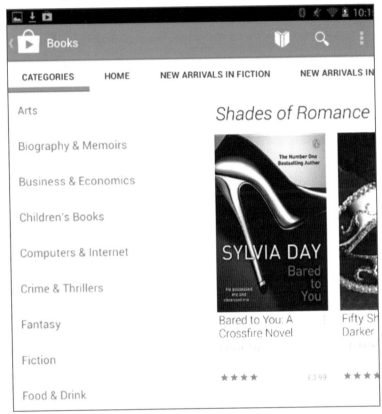

Alternatively you can search for a particular book after tapping the search icon shown on the right and above. Type the title of the book, replacing **Search Google Play** shown below. Or tap the microphone icon shown in the middle below and speak the title.

For example, a search for **Bradshaws Guide** produced numerous results, as shown in the small sample below. Tap a book cover for more details or to buy the book. Alternatively tap the small three dot menu shown below, to the right of the book title, to add the book to a wish list or buy it. Some of the publications on this particular subject are free.

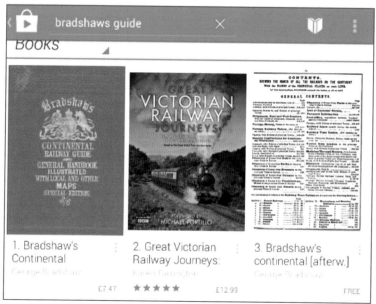

In order to make sure you can read a book offline, you may be asked to tap a pin icon on the book cover, when you are online. Then, for example, you will be able to read the book in Aeroplane Mode during a flight, if

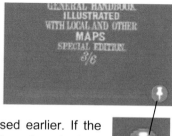

the airline permits this, as discussed earlier. If the book is available for reading offline, the pin icon appears vertical, as shown on the right.

Reading an eBook

Tap the Books app on the Favorites tray, or on the All Apps screen, to open My Library, as discussed on page 59. Then tap the cover of the book you want to read. The book opens on the screen at the first page. Scroll backwards and forwards through the pages by swiping to the left or right.

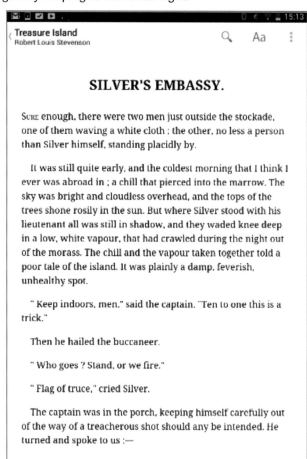

Tap anywhere on the screen to view information about the current page you are reading, as shown below.

Drag the blue bar to advance rapidly forward or backward through the book. A blue triangle marks the page you were previously reading.

The menu bar across the top of the eBook page, as shown above and on the previous page, includes the following icons:

Search for certain words and highlight them where they occur in the text.

Change the brightness, type size and typeface.

Open the menu shown on the right, which includes options to **bookmark** a page in the text.

This icon, also shown at the bottom left of the previous page, lists chapter headings, page numbers and bookmarks. You can view and return to the bookmarked pages after tapping this icon. You can also **Share** the book with someone else, using social networking or e-mail.

Read aloud on the menu at the bottom of the previous page turns the Nexus 7 into a *talking book*. The **Settings** option on the menu displays the window shown below. This includes options to turn **Read aloud** on when an **Accessibility** setting is on and to use the volume control key to turn pages.

Original pages shown on the menu at the bottom of the previous page displays a book in the style of the original paper edition of the book, as shown in the extract below.

CHAPTER XXV.

I STRIKE THE JOLLY ROGER.

I HAD scarce gained a position on the bowsprit, when the flying jib flapped and filled upon the other tack, with a report like a gun. The schooner trembled to her keel under the reverse; but next moment, the other sails

Access to eBooks and Other Media Offline

The Nexus 7 automatically stores all the eBooks (and other media such as music, etc.,) in your library in the clouds on the Internet. This makes them very rapidly available when you are connected to Wi-Fi. However, if you want to read the books *offline* (e.g. in Aeroplane Mode as discussed earlier, or where there is no Wi-Fi), the books, etc., need to be saved on the internal storage of the Nexus 7. Tap the **Play Books** icon on the Home Screen or on the Favorites tray shown on page 58. With the **My Library** screen selected, tap the small three dot menu icon to the right of the name of each book, as shown on the right and on the left below. This displays a small menu, as shown on the right below.

Tap **Keep on device**, shown above, to retain access to your eBooks, etc., when you are not connected to Wi-Fi.

Deleting eBooks and Other Media

Tap **Delete from library** shown above and below, to remove the eBook or music, etc., from your library in the clouds. The **Don't keep** option appears on the menu shown on the right, if an eBook or music, etc., has been previously saved on the internal storage of the Nexus 7, for reading offline. Tapping **Don't keep** removes the eBook or music, etc., from the internal storage of the Nexus 7.

The Kindle App for the Nexus 7

To read eBooks in the popular Kindle format, it's just a case of installing the Kindle app from the Google Play Store. Tap the Play Store shopping bag icon, shown on

the right and on the right of the Favorites tray. Then tap **APPS** and tap the magnifying glass search icon. Type **Kindle** into the search bar or tap the microphone icon and say **Kindle** to display a list of Kindle apps, as shown in the sample above.

Tap the Amazon Kindle app shown on the left above and tap **INSTALL** to put an icon, shown on the right, on your All Apps and Home Screens. Sign in with an e-mail address and password for an Amazon account or create a new account.

To start reading one of the Kindle books you already have, tap the front cover.

Tap **Store** at the top right of the screen to open the Amazon Book Store of over 2 million books. If you already have an account with Amazon, you can buy books very easily using **Buy Now with 1-Click**.

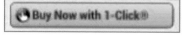

Magazines on the Nexus 7

The procedure for obtaining magazines is basically the same as for eBooks, as described on pages 59 to 61. Just select **MAGAZINES** in the Play Store and choose from a huge selection of magazines in various categories. You can

buy a single edition or take out a subscription for regular issues.

Managing Magazines

Options for managing magazines appear when you view the front cover of the magazine in My Library, as discussed on page 62 for eBooks. The note **On device** indicates that this magazine has been downloaded and saved on the internal storage of the Nexus 7. This is confirmed by the white vertical pin icon, as shown below.

The vertical white pin indicates that the magazine can be read offline, as in Aeroplane mode with Wi-Fi switched off. A grey pin at an angle indicates that the magazine cannot be read offline. A purple angled pin indicates that the magazine can be read offline but may be deleted to save space on the Nexus 7. The three dot menu icon shown on the right and above shows the following options: **Keep on device** or **Don't keep** and **Delete from library**.

Keep on device is used if you want to make a newly purchased magazine (or book), available offline, by saving it on the internal storage of the Nexus 7.

Don't keep appears when a magazine or book has already been saved on the internal storage and you may wish to remove it.

Delete from library removes a magazine or book from storage in the clouds, the default location on the Internet where all your files are automatically kept.

Reading a Magazine

With your magazine displayed in My Library, simply tap the front cover. Turn the pages of the magazine by swiping horizontally. Tap over a page and then tap the icon at the bottom of the screen, shown on the right, and on the left below, to display a contents list of the articles in the magazine.

Music on the Nexus 7

The methods used for obtaining and listening to music are very similar to those just described for books and magazines. Open the Play Store as described on page 59 and select **MUSIC**.

Then browse for the music you want, using the various **GENRES**, such as **Classical**, **Folk** or **Pop** and **TOP ALBUMS** or **TOP SONGS**, etc.

Alternatively tap the magnifying glass search icon, shown below, then enter the name of the record or artist. You can type the words or tap the microphone icon and speak them.

You can buy singles as shown on the right, or albums. Tap the cover to buy the single or album. Also shown is the familiar three dot menu which, in this example, has options to **Add to wishlist** or **Buy £0.99**.

After tapping to buy a piece of music it is added to your library in the clouds, as discussed earlier. Then it can be played after opening the music app by tapping the headset icon shown on the left, located on the All Apps screen.

The control bar along the bottom of the Nexus 7 music screen has the usual Play, Forward, Back and Pause buttons, as shown below at the bottom right. The volume control key on the side of the Nexus 7 is shown on page 12 of this book. Tap the three dot menu icon on the front cover to display a list of options, including **Keep on device**. This will save the music on your Nexus 7, not just in the clouds, allowing you to play the music when you are offline, i.e. not connected to the Internet.

Movies on the Nexus 7

The Play Store contains a range of movies and TV shows in various categories. Some can be bought or rented while others can only be rented. You may have to start watching a movie within 30 days of starting to rent it and the rental may expire 48 hours after you start watching it.

Tap **RENT** or **BUY** then select **PLAY** or **DOWNLOAD**.

To watch a movie you've bought or rented, tap the Movies icon shown on the right, which appears on the All Apps screen and by default on the Favorites tray.

Downloading for Offline Viewing – the Pin Icon

To make a movie watchable offline, tap the angled pin icon on the movie graphic, shown on the right. This starts downloading the movie. The pin icon starts to fill with colour and, when completely full, the download is complete. The pin icon is now white and vertical, as shown on the right. A notification should also be displayed when you swipe down from the top left-hand corner of the screen, as discussed on page 52.

The YouTube App

The Movies app discussed on the previous page allows you to buy or rent commercial films. In contrast, YouTube is a Web site, owned by Google, which provides a platform for ordinary people to share videos which they have recorded themselves. These can rapidly become very popular and are said to "go viral" when millions of people watch them around the world.

To launch YouTube, tap the icon shown on the right (Android 4.2) or the lower icon on the right (Android 4.3). The YouTube icon is found on the All Apps screen. The YouTube screen shows a long list of video clips which can be scrolled up and down by swiping. Swipe the graphics to the right to display the menu shown below on the left-hand side. There are recommendations of videos to watch, popular clips

currently **Trending** and **Live** coverage of major sporting and other events. To watch a video, tap the menu option such as **Trending** or **Cars** and, if necessary, scroll vertically to display the cover picture and title of the required video. Tap the picture to start the video. To pause a video, tap the screen.

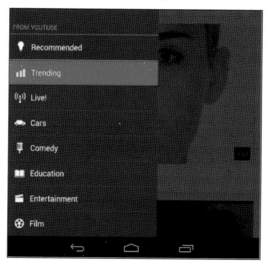

Live and Catchup Television and Radio

The Google Play Store includes the free BBC iPlayer app, as shown on the right. This can be obtained from the Play Store and installed on your Nexus 7 using the methods described on pages 36-39. Tap the icon shown on the right to open the BBC iPlayer as shown below.

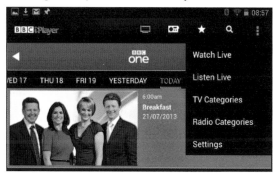

The row of icons on the upper right above enable you to switch between TV and radio, then to choose a channel. Tap the three dot menu shown on the right to display the above menu, which gives the options to watch or listen to live TV and radio. Otherwise go back and watch or listen to programs from the previous week, as shown below.

Nexus 7 Games

The Google Play Store contains lots of free and inexpensive games in various categories, as shown below.

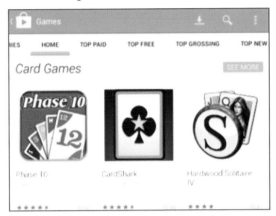

Games are installed as apps on your All Apps and Home Screens, as discussed on pages 36-39. To launch a game, tap its icon, as shown on the right.

You may wish to group all your games into one or more folders, as discussed on page 30. Tap the resulting circular folder icon to open the folder and give it a name. For quick access, the folder icon can be placed on the Favorites tray by sliding it into a gap created by sliding away another app, as discussed on page 29. In the example below, a games folder has been placed third from the left on the Favorites tray.

Streaming versus Downloading

Media such as photos, videos, movies, eBooks, etc., are held as *files* on the network computers of companies such as Google, Amazon, YouTube, Spotify and Netflix. Movie and video files can be extremely large and can take a long time to transfer over the Internet. Now, with faster broadband Internet, it is more feasible, to make a copy of videos, etc., on your Nexus 7.

However, as mentioned, movie, video and music files that you buy or rent from the Play Store or Kindle Store are not automatically saved locally on the Nexus 7. They remain in the clouds on the Internet and you must be online to enjoy them.

Streaming

A media file is ***temporarily*** transmitted to your computer over the Internet and you access it in *real time*. A copy is ***not saved*** on the Nexus 7. You need to be connected to the Internet every time you want to access this file. A *buffer* may be used to temporarily store "chunks" of the video, etc., to guard against interruptions in the streaming process. You will only be able to access the streamed media when you are online.

If a file is ***not saved*** on your Nexus 7 you may see this angled-pin icon on the music, movie, or eBook graphic in My Library.

Downloading

A copy of a media file is transferred over the Internet and **saved** on the internal storage of the Nexus 7. You can access this eBook, video, movie, etc., at any time in the future, without being connected to the Internet. Downloaded files are needed if you want to use media in Aeroplane mode or in situations where there is no Wi-Fi. Use the menu option **Keep on device** to make sure files are saved on the internal storage of the Nexus 7.

Files downloaded and saved on your Nexus 7 for later viewing offline display a vertical pin icon as shown on the right.

Browsing the Web

Introduction

The Nexus 7 gives us access to millions of Web pages, containing the latest information on any subject you care to think of. Much of this information is of the highest quality, from respected academic, scientific and professional sources.

The Google Chrome Web browser enables you to search the millions of Web pages quickly and easily and displays the results in an attractive and readable format. The Google search app is the world's leading Web search program on all platforms – tablet, laptop and desktop computers. So it's not surprising that the Google Nexus 7 is an ideal tool for browsing the Internet. In my opinion this alone justifies the modest purchase price of the Nexus 7, not to mention its many other functions such as news, social networking and entertainment, discussed elsewhere in this book.

Some of the main functions of Google Chrome are:

- To search for and display information after entering or speaking *keywords* into the Google search engine.

- To access Web pages after entering their *address* such as **www.babanibooks.com** into the browser.

- To move between Web pages by tapping *links* or *hyperlinks* on a Web page and move forward and backwards between Web pages.

- To *bookmark* Web pages for revisiting at a later time.

Launching Google Chrome

To launch Google Chrome, tap its icon on the All Apps screen or on the Favorites tray, shown below.

The **Welcome to Google Chrome** screen opens, as shown below. Tap **Take a tour** to view several pages of notes to help you get started.

The search bar across the top of the screen is the place to start your Web browsing activities. Here you enter either the address of a Web site or *keywords* which should pinpoint the subject you are interested in.

Entering the Address of a Web Site

Every Web site has a unique address, known as its *URL*, or *Uniform Resource Locator*. A typical Web address is:

www.babanibooks.com.

Type the URL into the search bar, as shown below and tap the **Go** key on the on-screen keyboard.

For a complicated address you may need to enter the URL in full. However, in practice you'll often find you don't need to be too pedantic; simply entering **babanibooks**, for example, will lead you to the required Web site. If you've visited a site before, it may appear in a list of suggested Web sites which pops up to save you typing the full address.

Instead of typing the URL, as discussed above, you might prefer to tap the microphone icon shown on the right, then speak the Web address.

After entering the address of the Web site into the search bar and pressing **Go**, the Web site's Home Page should quickly open on the screen, as shown in the extract below.

The Keyword Search

This is used for finding out about a particular subject rather than visiting a Web site whose address you know, as discussed on the previous page. The Web appears to contain pages covering every conceivable subject. For example, suppose you were interested in the history of England and Scotland and wanted to find out about the Border Reivers, who were a major part of the Border's turbulent past. Simply enter **border reivers** into the Google Chrome search bar, as shown below. (There's no need to use capital letters when entering search criteria — **Border Reivers** or **border reivers** produce the same results).

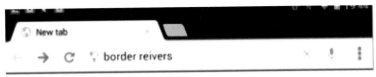

After tapping the **Go** key on the on-screen keyboard, the screen displays a list of Google search results, as shown below.

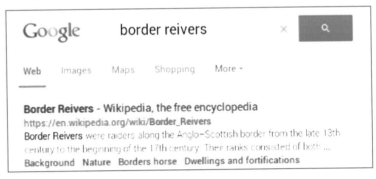

Only the top search result is shown above in blue but a search often yields millions of results. Google places the most significant results near the top of the list. Some results may be irrelevant to a particular search. For example, historians studying the Border Reivers may not be particularly interested in the Web site of the Border Reivers Rambling Club which might appear in the results.

Each of the blue headings on a search result represents a *link* to a Web page containing the keywords, Border Reivers in this example. Tap a link to have a look at the Web site.

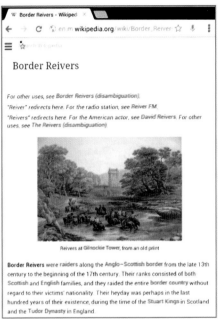

Surfing the Net

On the Web page shown above, some words are highlighted in blue. These are *links* which can be tapped to open further Web pages. Each new page will probably have lots of further links, so tapping these will open a succession of Web pages.

Try typing a few diverse keywords into Google Chrome and see how easy it is to find good information on virtually any subject. Here's a few to get you started:

halebop	histamine	entrevaux
making elderberry wine	samuel johnson	thatching a roof
florence nightingale	hadron collider	shearing a sheep

The Internet is surely the world's largest and most up-to-date encyclopaedia covering almost every known subject, no matter how bizarre. At a more practical level, Google Chrome is probably the DIY enthusiast's best friend. Type any DIY task, such as **mending a puncture**, for example, and numerous Web sites offer helpful advice, often including step-by-step videos.

Previously Visited Pages

As you move between Web pages, you may wish to briefly revisit a page. The back and forward buttons shown on the right and below allow you to quickly move between recently visited pages. Tapping the circular arrow button on the right and below reloads the latest version of a Web page. (For speed, the Chrome browser may load an earlier version of a Web page).

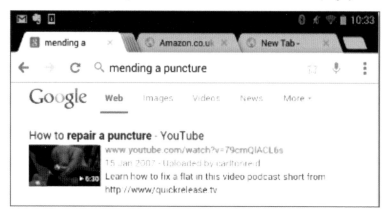

As you move forward or back between Web pages, the keywords from each search, such as **shearing a sheep**, are displayed on the tab at the top left of the screen, as shown above and below.

Tabbed Browsing

When you do a search in Google Chrome and then proceed to surf the Web, as described earlier, there is only one tab displaying the current Web page, as described at the bottom of the previous page. However, Chrome allows you to open each Web page in a tab of their own, so that all the tabs are visible along the top of the screen, as shown in the example below.

This makes it easy to move straight to a particular Web page, rather than moving through them all one at a time using the back and forward buttons. Tap a tab to open that Web page. With a large number of Web pages open, the tabs may be stacked on top of each other and can be moved around by sliding or gently swiping left or right.

Opening a Web Page in Its Own New Tab

Tap the **New tab** icon shown on the right and below.

A **New tab** appears, as shown above on the right, with the search bar ready for you to enter your search criteria by typing or speaking. After carrying out the search and selecting a Web page from the results, this page appears on its own tab. The search criteria, in this case **green woodpecker**, appear on the top of the tab, as shown below.

Using the Google App

In the previous examples, Google Chrome was opened by tapping its icon on the Favorites tray. You can also launch Chrome after tapping the Google icon shown on the right, on the All Apps screen. Then enter the search criteria, such as **honey buzzard sightings** in this example, in the Google search bar, as shown below.

Tap on a link in the search results to open a Web page you want to look at. The Web page opens in Google Chrome, in a new tab of its own, **Honey Buzzard...**, in this example, as shown below.

To switch to another Web page from a previous search, simply tap its tab, such as **mending a puncture**, partly shown above.

Closing a Tab

Close a tab by tapping the cross, as shown on the right below.

Bookmarking a Web Page

You can create a series of *bookmarks* so that you can quickly return to your favourite Web pages at any time in the future. With the required Web page open on the screen, tap the star-shaped bookmark icon as shown on the right and on the right of the search bar below.

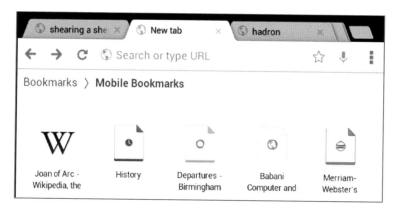

The **Add Bookmark** window opens, allowing you to name the bookmark or accept the name provided by default. Tap **Save** to add the Web page to the **Mobile Bookmarks** page. To view the bookmarks, tap the three dot menu icon shown on the right and then tap **Bookmarks** on the drop-down menu.

Bookmarks 〉 **Mobile Bookmarks**

W	•	○	◎	⊜
Joan of Arc - Wikipedia, the	History	Departures - Birmingham	Babani Computer and	Merriam-Webster's

To open one of the bookmarked Web pages, tap its icon on the **Bookmarks** page, as shown above. Press and hold a bookmark icon to display the menu shown on the right, including options to edit and delete a bookmark or add a bookmark to your Home screen.

Open in new tab

Open in Incognito tab

Edit bookmark

Delete bookmark

Add to Home screen

Displaying Your Browsing History

Google Chrome keeps a record, in chronological order, of all the Web pages you've recently visited. Surprisingly there isn't a button to display the History feature. However it can easily be displayed by typing **chrome://history/** into the search bar.

When you tap **Go**, your **History** list is displayed, as shown below.

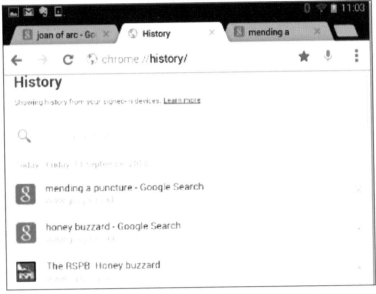

To save time when opening your History, instead of entering **Chrome://history/** into the search bar, create a bookmark, as shown on the right. Creating a bookmark is described on page 83.

History

There are options to **CLEAR ALL BROWSING DATA** and **Search history**.

Communication and Social Networking

Introduction

This chapter describes the various ways the Nexus 7 can be used to communicate electronically. The main topics are:

Electronic Mail or E-mail

Used by businesses and friends and families to send messages, documents and photos all over the world.

Skype

Free worldwide *voice* and *video* calls between computers.

Facebook

The most popular *social networking* Web site. Enter your personal *profile* and *timeline* and make *online friends* to share news with people having similar interests.

Twitter

Another very popular social networking site, based on short text messages (*140 characters maximum*) which can be read by anyone who choses to follow the originator, who may be a celebrity, company or a member of the public.

Two more social networks are discussed briefly at the end of this chapter. **Google+** is a network for sharing text messages, photos, videos and video chat. **LinkedIn** is a network used by individuals and companies for developing employment and business opportunities.

Electronic Mail

Gmail is Google's electronic mail service. It's currently the most popular, ahead of other well-known services such as Microsoft's Hotmail and Outlook.com and Yahoo! Mail. Gmail is powerful yet easy to use and very good at filtering out "spam", the unsolicited junk mail or advertising that can waste a lot of your time.

Gmail is used for creating, sending and receiving text messages over the Internet, as an alternative to sending letters by the traditional post. *Replies* can easily be sent to the original sender of a message you've received and, if necessary, to all other recipients of the original message. An e-mail can be *forwarded* to anyone else you think may be interested.

You can maintain an *address book* for all your contacts and *import* into it files of contacts from other e-mail services.

An e-mail message can include photos and documents, known as *attachments,* "clipped" to the message and sent with it.

Gmail is a Web-based e-mail service, so you can access your electronic correspondence from anywhere in the world. All you need is a connection to the Internet and your Gmail username and password, as discussed on page 16. If someone else has already used your chosen e-mail address, you may need to add numbers, such as **stellaaustin86@gmail.com**, for example.

There are two e-mail apps on the All Apps screen of the Nexus 7. The yellow **Email** app, shown on the right, is used for accessing any of your other e-mail accounts, such as Hotmail or Outlook.com.

Gmail is opened by tapping the lower icon shown on the right. When you first start using Gmail, an almost blank screen appears with just the words **No conversations** in the middle. Once you've been using Gmail for a while, there'll be plenty of "conversations", i.e. your messages and the corresponding replies.

Creating a Message

Tap the **Compose** icon shown on the top right of the screen, as shown on the right and below.

The **Compose** screen opens, as shown below. Enter the main recipient's e-mail address in the **To** bar. Tapping **+CC/BCC** shown on the right below opens two new lines in which to enter further recipients. These can receive either **Carbon Copies** or **Blind Carbon Copies**. BCC recipients don't know who else has received a copy.

Adding an Attachment

Tap the icon shown on the right and on the previous page. You are then given a choice of locations from which to select the photo, document or some other type of file which you wish to attach to the message. This might be a document saved in My Drive (discussed shortly) or a picture in the Gallery, for example. Tap the required photo, etc., and the attachments should appear on the bottom of the e-mail, as shown on the previous page. The attachments in this example are the swan photo and a PDF document called **Riviera.pdf**.

Sending an E-mail

When all the text has been entered and any attachments added, tap the **Send** button on the bar across the top of the screen.

Receiving an E-mail

The e-mail will be available for reading by the recipient almost immediately, as soon as they open their *Inbox*.

The paper clip icon on the right and above indicates that an attachment has been sent. Tap anywhere on the message header above to open the complete message.

Tap the small photo to open it fully on the screen. To open an attached document, tap its name, as shown on the right. You are presented with a choice of several apps with which to open the document.

Skype

This is a service which allows you to make free *voice* and *video* calls all over the world. If you often make telephone calls to people abroad using a mobile phone or landline, using Skype on a computer such as a Nexus 7 can save you a lot of money. Calls between two computers are absolutely free. If you use your Nexus 7 to call a mobile phone or landline there is a charge, for which you need a Skype account with some credit in it.

Hundreds of millions of people use Skype to make voice and video calls. You can also send photographs and instant text messages. The Nexus 7 is already fully equipped for Skype, with a suitable webcam and built in microphone and speakers. The Skype app in the Google Play Store is free and can be installed as described in Chapter 3.

Start Skype by tapping its icon on the All Apps screen, as shown on the right. Then you need to sign in using an existing Skype username and password or a Microsoft account. Alternatively, create a new Skype account. When you sign in, contacts from your address book are displayed.

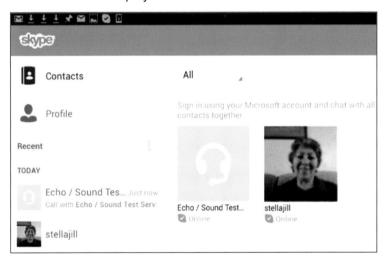

The **Echo/Sound Test** shown at the bottom of the previous page asks you to record and replay a few words to check that your microphone and sound are working correctly.

Making a Skype Call

Any contacts currently online are displayed with a tick, as shown on the right and on the previous page. These people can be contacted by a voice call, including video if they've a camera connected.

Tap the name or thumbnail of a contact who is currently online. A screen opens with two icons to initiate a call, as shown on the right. The left-hand icon is used to record a video message. Tapping the phone icon on the right above starts a call. This will be a two-way video call if your contact has a camera attached to their computer.

Receiving a Call

When someone "Skypes" you, the Nexus 7 will emit the distinctive ring of a Skype call and the name of the person calling you appears on the screen. Tap the green phone icon shown on the right to accept the call and make a connection.

If the other person has a camera connected, you can see their face on your screen. The icon on the extreme left below displays the image on the full screen. The next icon (also shown on the right), shows that the caller does not have a camera connected. The microphone icon shows that the participants can hear each other. The **+** icon launches the Text Chat feature. The red phone icon ends a call.

Facebook

This Web site started off in America, as a way for students to introduce themselves and make friends with other students. Now Facebook is the biggest social network, with over a billion users all over the world. To join Facebook, you must be aged over 13 years and have a valid e-mail address. You can access Facebook on the Nexus 7 using the Facebook app, installed from the Play Store, as discussed in Chapter 3. Or you can open Google Chrome and enter **www.facebook.com** in the address bar. Either way you will need to *sign up* for a new Facebook account and in future *sign in* with your e-mail address and password.

First you create your own *Profile* in the form of a *Timeline*, as shown on the lower right. This can include personal details such as your schools, employers and hobbies and interests. This information is used by Facebook to provide lists of people who have similar interests or backgrounds to yourself. This list also includes people who are in your e-mail address book. You then send invitations to anyone you want to be your Facebook *friends*. Anyone who accepts will be able to exchange news, information, photos and videos with you.

The term *friends* on Facebook may include close personal friends and family but it might also include people you don't really know. Care should be taken when making friends on Facebook, especially if you've posted your contact details.

Security and Privacy

The *audience selector* icon shown on the right appears against the items of personal information in your profile. Tapping this icon displays a drop-down menu, as shown on the right, enabling you to set the level of privacy for each item, ranging from **Public** to **Only me**. **Public** means *everyone* can see the information, including people you don't know.

Status Updates

These are used to post your latest information and news and usually consist of a short text message and probably one or more photos. Tap **Status** on the top left of the screen in the Nexus 7 Facebook app, or if using Facebook in Google Chrome, type your update straight into the **What's on your mind?** box. An icon at the bottom of the screen allows you to insert a photo stored on the Nexus 7, as discussed in Chapter 9. There is also an icon to set the audience who can receive this update.

After you tap **Post**, shown above, your friends will receive the update in an area of Facebook known as their *News Feed*.

Twitter

Like Facebook, twitter is a social networking Web site used by hundreds of millions of people. There is a free app for Twitter in the Nexus 7 Play Store which can be installed, as discussed in Chapter 3. You can also use the original Web version of Twitter by entering **www.twitter.com** into Google Chrome. Signing up to Twitter is free. Once signed up you can either use your e-mail address and password to sign in or you can enter your Twitter username such as **@jimsmith**. Some of the main features of Twitter are:

- Twitter is a Web site used for posting text messages, known as *tweets*, of up to 140 characters in length.

- You can include a 160 character *personal profile* on your Twitter page.

- Photographs can be posted with a tweet.

- Twitter is based on people *following*, i.e. reading the tweets of other people, such as celebrities, politicians and companies marketing their products or services.

- You can follow anyone you like, but you can't choose who follows you. If you have no followers, anything you post on Twitter will remain unread. You could encourage your friends and family to follow you and each other on Twitter, to share your latest news.

- *Hashtags*, such as *#climatechange*, for example, make it simple for other people to find all the tweets on a particular subject. The hashtag is included within a tweet. Tapping the hashtag displays all the tweets on that subject, which might be a campaign or a debate.

- If you like a tweet, it can be *retweeted* to all of your followers, together with comments of your own.

- You can send *replies* to a tweet.

Sending a Tweet

Tap the quill icon shown on the right and on the **Home**
screen in the screenshot at the bottom of this page. The
following screen opens displaying the words **What's
happening?** Replace these with your own message.

A counter at the top right shows that 37 of the maximum 140
characters are still available to be used. An icon at the bottom of
the tweet creation screen, shown on the left below, enables you
to include your current location from a pop-up map. The camera
icon is used to take a photo and include it in the tweet. The icon
on the right is for including photos already stored on the Nexus 7.
(Photos are discussed in Chapter 9).

When the tweet is finished, tap TWEET shown in the tweet
creation box at the top of this page. Your followers will see your
tweet in their Home screen, as shown below.

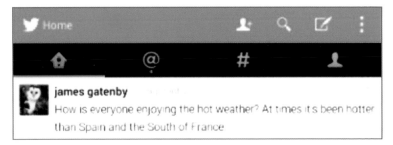

Responding to a Tweet

If the reader taps a tweet, the following toolbar is displayed.

These icons enable you to respond to a tweet in various ways. Reading from left to right, they are:

Reply, **Retweet**, mark as **Favorite** and **Share** with other people.

Viewing Photographs

If a tweet includes a photo, the reader of the tweet sees a link embedded in the text, such as **pic.twitter.com/n8fRQHKbyD** shown below. This link is automatically created by Twitter.

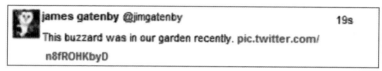

Tap the blue link shown above to open the photo on the screen as shown on the right.

LinkedIn

This is a social network for professionals, with over 250 million users all over the world. You can use LinkedIn to create your own network of useful contacts. Users enter their *profile* consisting of photographs, experience and qualifications, etc. Companies have access to users' profiles and can target job advertisements at suitable candidates. Companies can also use LinkedIn to explore and develop new business opportunities.

There is a free app for LinkedIn in the Google Play Store, as discussed in Chapter 3.

Google+

Although Facebook and Twitter seem to grab all the headlines, *Google+* is also a very popular social network, pre-installed on the Nexus 7. After tapping the **g+** icon on the All Apps screen, sign in to your Gmail account and enter a short profile, including your photo. After tapping **Done**, the main screen opens, already showing lots of messages and photos.

Tapping the red **g+** icon in the top left-hand corner of the screen displays the menu shown below. The **Hangout** option enables you to have *video chats* with your contacts.

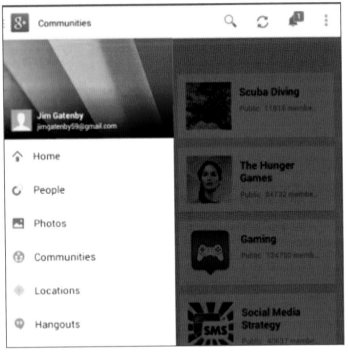

To start posting a message, tap the **Write** pencil icon at the bottom right of the screen.

Google Drive
and Google Docs

Google Drive

This app brings all the advantages of *cloud computing* to the Nexus 7. If, like me, you also use laptop and desktop computers, the advantages are enormous. The Google Drive app is free from the Nexus 7 Play Store and when installed is opened by the icon shown on the right. You can also download and install the free Google Drive application on laptop and desktop computers.

In the past, if I wanted to transfer documents from the desktop machine in my home office to a laptop in the house, one of the following methods was needed:

- Transfer the files using a storage medium, such as a flash drive or CD, etc.

- E-mail the files to myself as attachments.

- Copy the files across the home network. This process requires both computers to be up and running.

With Google Drive installed on all your computers, anything you enter in the Nexus 7, such as a word processing document, automatically gets copied to a Google Web server computer "in the clouds". From there it is automatically downloaded to your other machines, as soon as they are switched on. The files are said to have been *synced* or *synchronised* to your other computers.

Using Google Drive to store all your documents in the clouds has several important advantages:

- If you always save your files to the Drive folder, all your computers always have the latest editions of your files.

- You don't need to worry about making separate backup copies — your files are professionally managed and backed up on the server computers "in the clouds".

- If you log on with your Gmail password, you can access your files anywhere in the world.

- With your permission, friends or colleagues can collaborate on the editing of the same document and everyone sees the latest amended edition.

If you have a laptop or desktop PC and want to sync documents with your Nexus 7, log onto **www.google.co.uk** on the laptop or desktop machine. Then select the **Apps** icon on the top right of the screen, shown here on the right. From the drop -down window which appears, select the **Drive** icon, shown on the right, to open the window shown below. Then click **Download Google Drive for PC** as shown on the blue button on the left below.

A Google Drive folder is created on each computer on which you install Google Drive. New and edited files in a Drive folder are synced to the Drive folders on all your other computers, such as the Nexus 7. Google allows users 15 GB of free storage space in the clouds for Drive files, Gmail and photos.

Google Docs

This is the document creation part of Google Drive. Traditionally, users of laptop and desktop computers bought software such as Microsoft Word and Excel for producing reports and financial spreadsheets, etc. While excellent products in themselves, they contain a lot of features which many people never need. These packages at one time cost hundreds of pounds and could only be installed on one, or perhaps three, computers unless a multi-user licence was purchased. This software is traditionally bought in boxes, together with an installation CD or DVD.

Google Docs has moved the goal posts when it comes to office software. Once you've installed Google Drive you immediately have access to Google Docs, which is free *web-based software* and includes word processing and spreadsheeet apps. So this software will also be available on any computer with Google Drive installed, after you've signed in with your Gmail username and password.

Although the word processor and spreadsheet software in Google Drive may not be as full of features as Word or Excel, they are quite adequate for most purposes. As mentioned elsewhere, if you want to write a 300 page thesis or typeset a book (such as this one), you'd probably want to use a desktop publishing application on a laptop or desktop computer.

Creating a New Document

Tap the Drive icon on the All Apps screen, shown on the right. The **My Drive** screen opens with the following menu bar across the top.

Tap the **+** icon, shown above, to open a new document, as shown on the next page.

Word Processing Using Google Docs

The **Add new** menu opens, as shown on the right, allowing you to create a new word processing document or a spreadsheet. You can also create a new folder within the Drive folder and upload files. **Scan** (Android 4.3 only) launches a camera allowing you to scan a document or take a photo. These are saved in the Drive folder. Selecting **Document** on the right above opens a window into which you type a title for a new word processing document, before tapping **OK**.

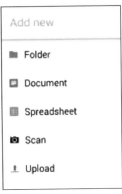

The file is created and a blank word processing screen opens, ready for you to start typing the text, as shown below.

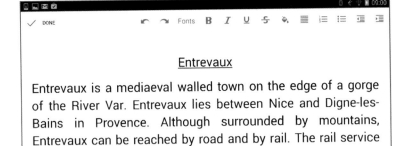

Landscape mode gives a better view of the word processing menu bar at the top of the screen. As discussed on page 102, this is also true for the spreadsheet menu bar.

As shown along the menu bar at the top of the word processing screenshot on page 100, all the main tools are present, such as undo, redo, bold, italic, underline, justification and different font sizes and styles. You can also apply bullets and numbering and text in various colours. Tap a word twice to select or highlight it ready for formatting or editing.

When you've finished entering and editing the text, tap **DONE** in the top left-hand corner and the document is saved automatically in the clouds.

Synchronisation Between Computers

The document is synced to your other computers and you can open it on them as soon as you sign into Gmail and open the Drive folder. The Entrevaux note created on the Nexus 7, is shown below, synced to my laptop PC computer. It also syncs to any desktop PCs and iPads with Google Drive installed.

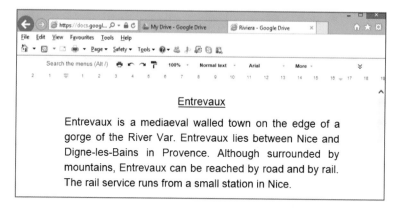

Free Word Processing Apps

The Play Store, includes the popular *Writer* from James McMinn, while *Kingsoft Office* includes both word processing and spreadsheet apps. *Evernote* is very popular for keeping notes, making lists and handling photos.

Using the Google Docs Spreadsheet

Tap the **+** icon, shown below, to open a new document, as shown on the next page.

Then select **Spreadsheet** from the **Add new** menu, as shown on page 100. A blank spreadsheet opens ready for you to start entering the data, as shown below.

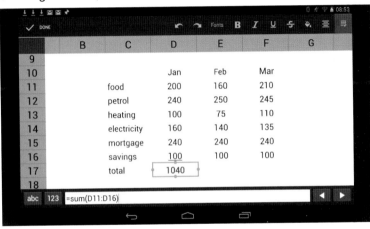

It's probably more convenient to hold the Nexus 7 in landscape mode as shown above. If necessary, in order to display landscape view, swipe down from the top right of the screen and make sure **AUTO ROTATE** appears in the Quick Settings panel, not **ROTATION LOCKED**, as discussed on pages 48 and 49.

This enables you to see all of the icons on the menu bar across the top of the screen, without having to scroll horizontally. Tap to select a cell, then use the keyboard to enter or edit data, using the formula bar at the bottom of the screen, showing here:

=sum(D11:D16).

As shown on the previous page, the spreadsheet app has the normal text formatting tools, such as undo, redo, bold, italic, underline, etc., and text in various fonts, sizes and colours. Columns or rows can be selected for editing by tapping at the top of a column or at the extreme left of a row. Tap **Done** at the top left of the screen to save the spreadsheet in the clouds.

Managing Your Google Docs

The word processing and spreadsheet docs that you create are saved in the clouds as files on a Google server computer. The files are listed on the **My Drive** page on the Nexus 7, when you first sign into **Gmail** and launch **Drive**. To open a particular file, tap its thumbnail, as shown below.

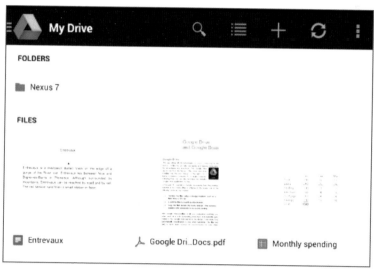

As shown above, **My Drive** in this example displays the thumbnails for the **Entrevaux** document and a **Monthly spending** spreadsheet. In the centre is a thumbnail for this chapter, which was created on a PC computer in PDF format and dropped into the Drive folder on the PC. The chapter then synced automatically from the PC to the Nexus 7 via the clouds.

Press and hold a thumbnail for a file in **My Drive** as shown on the previous page and you are presented with the following menu, including options to **Remove**, **Rename** and **Print** the file.

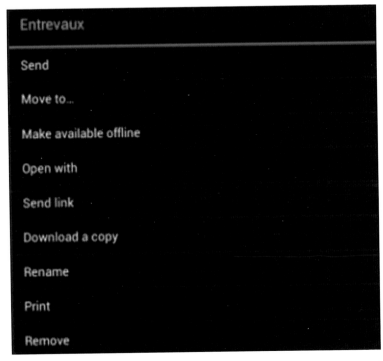

Make available offline saves a copy of the file on the Internal storage of the Nexus 7, so it can be accessed when you are not connected to the Internet. Otherwise the file will only exist in the clouds for viewing online, i.e. over the Internet.

For entering a lot of text or numbers, you can use a separate physical keyboard, as discussed in Chapter 2. Alternatively, tap the microphone icon on the on-screen keyboard and *speak* the data.

Transferring Files from a PC to a Nexus 7

Files can be transferred to a Nexus 7 from a PC or Apple laptop or desktop computer. Simply drag and drop the files onto the Google Drive folder on the laptop or desktop machine. Then the files are synced automatically to your Nexus 7 via the clouds.

The above example shows two files on the left which have been synced from my PC to the Nexus 7, after copying them into the Drive folder on the PC. When you tap the **begonias** thumbnail shown above, the photograph opens on the full screen of the Nexus 7. The middle thumbnail above is a PDF file of this chapter. A choice of apps is presented to deal with the PDF file.

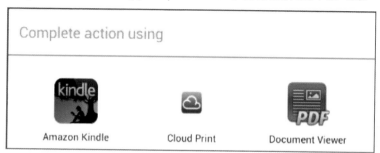

Tapping the **Riviera** thumbnail on the top right above opens the note about Entrevaux, created on the Nexus 7, discussed earlier.

Both the Nexus 7 Amazon Kindle app (on the left below) and the PDF Document Viewer, on the right, successfully opened the PDF file which has been synced from the PC.

Amazon Kindle   **PDF Document Viewer**

I also placed in the Drive folder on the PC, a copy of this chapter which had been saved on the PC in Microsoft Publisher format, **.pub**. Although it was successfully synced across to the Nexus 7, when you tap the thumbnail, the following message appears.

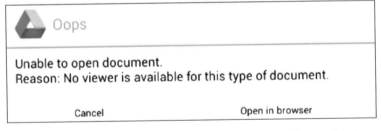

Files from a PC can be synced and opened on a Nexus 7 if they are saved in a common file format such as PDF or JPEG (.jpg). As shown above, the Nexus 7 cannot open a file unless it has suitable viewing software installed. However, PCs with software such as Microsoft Word and Publisher can save documents in the PDF format, enabling them to be opened on the Nexus 7.

Cloud Printing from the Nexus 7

Google Cloud Print is an app which allows you to output your documents to paper. Google state that you can use Cloud Print from anywhere and print across the Web to any printer.

If the icon for the app doesn't appear on your All Apps screen, it can be downloaded free from the Play Store, as described in Chapter 3.

If you already have a *Cloud Ready* printer which connects to the Web without being attached to a computer, this shouldn't need any setting up.

If you have a printer connected to a laptop or desktop PC, this is referred to as a *Classic* printer and needs to be set up in the Google Chrome Web browser as discussed below.

The setting up of a classic printer is done on a laptop or desktop computer connected to a printer and with Google Chrome installed. Open Google Chrome and make sure you are signed in with your Gmail address and password. This Gmail account will need to be used each time you use Cloud Print.

Open the Chrome menu by tapping or clicking the icon shown on the right and in context on the screen below.

From the menu select **Settings** and then scroll down the screen and at the bottom select **Show advanced settings**. Scroll down the next screen and under **Google Cloud Print** select **Add printers**. Select the printer you wish to use, as shown on the next page.

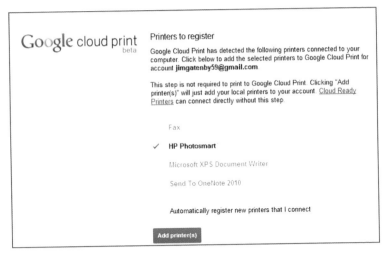

After selecting the printer, tap or click the **Add printer(s)** button shown in blue above. You should now see a message saying you're ready to start using Cloud Print with the current Google Account. There's also an option to **Manage your printers**.

Printing a Document Using Google Cloud Print

With the document displayed as a thumbnail in **My Drive** on the Nexus 7, as shown on page 105, press and hold the thumbnail. Then select **Print**, tap the required printer, set the number of copies, etc., and tap the **Print** button, as shown below, top right.

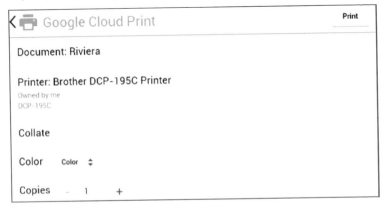

Working with Photos and Other Files

Introduction

You may need to transfer files from the Nexus 7 to another computer. Or you may have files on a laptop or desktop computer that you want to transfer to the Nexus 7. The following methods are available:

- As discussed in Chapter 8, files saved in Google Drive on the Nexus 7 are automatically synchronised to any other computers with Google Drive installed.

- Photos on a camera's SD card and various files types on a *flash drive* can be imported into the Nexus 7 using a special USB cable. A suitable app such as the *Nexus Media Importer* needs to be installed from the Play Store.

- Using the battery charging cable provided, connect the Nexus 7 to a laptop or desktop computer. Then use the File Manager on the laptop or desktop machine to manage files and copy them to and from the Nexus 7.

Please Note: At the time of writing there have been some difficulties importing files from SD cards and flash drives to some Nexus 7 machines using Android 4.3 Jelly Bean. If necessary, this problem can be overcome by importing the files first to a laptop or desktop machine. Then transferring them to the Nexus 7, using Google Drive or a USB cable as described in this chapter and in Chapter 8.

Importing Photos from an SD Card

As shown on page 20 and 24, the only extra hardware you need is the SD card reader and a cheap OTG USB cable. If you simply plug the SD card into the reader and connect the cable to the Nexus 7, nothing happens. You need to install a suitable app such as the Nexus Media Importer, available free in the Play Store and installed as described in Chapter 3.

After connecting the card reader, tap **OK** in response to **Open Nexus Media Importer when this USB device is connected?** The screen shown below appears, displaying thumbnails of all the photos on the SD card or just those in a particular folder. Scroll down, if necessary, to find the required photograph and tap its name. The photo appears as shown below.

The Play icon shown on the right and near the top right of the main screenshot on the previous page, displays the photos as a slide show. The icon on the right and on the previous page presents the photos in full screen mode.

The **Copy** icon shown on the right and above lets you save the selected photos in the **Pictures** folder in the **Internal storage** of the Nexus 7.

Tapping the **Share** icon shown on the right and above, allows you to send copies of the photo to numerous destinations such as your e-mail and social networking contacts. You can also send a copy to My Drive, as shown below, then view it whenever you want to.

Press and hold a photo, as shown above and a menu appears with various file management options such as **Send** (to destinations such as e-mail and social networking contacts), **Remove**, **Open with** (a particular app or program), **Rename**, **Move to...**, **Print** and **Make available offline**.

Importing Files from a Flash Drive

You may have other types of file, apart from photos, which you wish to import to the Nexus 7. For example, they may be on a *USB flash drive*, also known as a *memory stick*, as shown on the right. Like the SD card reader, the flash drive plugs  into the special micro USB cable discussed earlier and shown on page 24. The Nexus File Importer has options to import various file types such as **PHOTOS** and **DOCS** and to open **FOLDERS**, as shown below. Here the folder **MS Files** on the flash drive, has a *.doc* file (Word file 1997-2003), and *.docx* (Word file 2007 onwards). Also found on the flash drive is a *.xlsx* file (Excel spreadsheet), shown below.

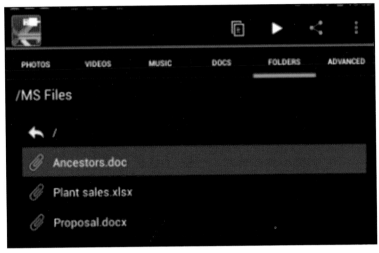

After selecting a file and tapping the Play button shown on the right and above, all being well, you are presented with a choice of apps installed on the Nexus 7 that can open that type of file. For example, the **Document Viewer** and **Kingsoft Office** shown on the next page can open Microsoft Word and Excel files, amongst others.

Opening Files from a PC on the Nexus 7

You may initially be unable to open some files which you import using the Nexus Media Importer. However, apps for viewing various files are available in the Play Store and these can be installed on the Nexus 7, as discussed in Chapter 3. For example, the freely available Kingsoft Office can open Microsoft file formats such as .doc, .docx, and .xlsx files and also .pdf files.

Both the Document Viewer and Kingsoft Office, which were already installed on my Nexus 7, were able to open the three types of file on the flash drive shown in

Document Viewer   Kingsoft Office

the screenshot on the previous page, i.e. .doc, .xlsx and .docx.

Microsoft Word File (.doc) opened on the Nexus 7

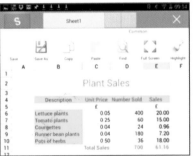

Microsoft Excel File (.xlsx) opened on the Nexus 7

The two screenshots above show the Word and Excel files opened on the Nexus 7 screen in Kingsoft Office. This excellent free app in the Play Store also allows you to use the Nexus 7 to *edit* and *save* files which were originally created on a PC. As its name implies, the Document Viewer allows you to use the Nexus 7 to read files which have been created on other computers, but doesn't permit editing.

Managing the Nexus 7 from a PC Computer

The Nexus 7 doesn't have its own *file manager* for deleting, copying, renaming files, etc. If you have a laptop or desktop computer, you can to use the file manager on this computer to manage the files on the Nexus 7. Connect the Nexus 7 to the laptop or desktop using the USB charging cable provided with a new Nexus 7. On a Windows PC, the Nexus 7 appears like a disc drive in the file manager, known as File Explorer or the Windows Explorer.

The extract on the right shows the **Nexus 7** listed on a laptop computer in the File Explorer in Windows 8. Double-clicking the name **Nexus 7** in the list displays the **Internal storage** of the Nexus 7, as if it's another disc drive, here showing **23.9GB** free out of a maximum of **27.5GB**. (The nominal 32GB quoted for the bigger Nexus 7 also includes the Jelly Bean operating system).

Double-clicking on the **Internal storage** image above displays all the folders on the Nexus 7. Each folder can be opened by double -clicking, such as the **Pictures** folder listed below.

> This PC ▸ Nexus 7 ▸ Internal storage ▸ Pictures

Right-click a file in the file manager window of the PC to open the menu shown on the right. This includes options to use the PC to **Delete**, **Edit**, **Copy** and **Rename** files on the Nexus 7. Files can be copied to and from the Nexus 7, by dragging and dropping.

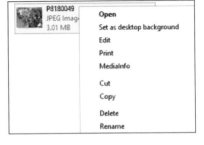

Cameras on the Nexus 7

Earlier versions of the Nexus 7 have one front facing camera. This camera launches automatically when needed in applications such as video calls with Skype. To take general photos with the forward facing camera you need to install an app such as *Camera Nexus 7 (official)* from the Play Store.

The latest Nexus 7 (Android Jelly Bean 4.3) has both forward and backward facing cameras, making it easier to take various photos and videos of people and objects. To take a general photograph on the new Nexus 7, tap the icon shown on the right, on the All Apps screen. This opens the new backward facing camera. Then another small camera icon allows you to select either a photo or a video. Tap the blue circle at the bottom of the screen to take the photo or video. Images are stored in the **Camera** folder, accessed by tapping the **Gallery** icon shown on the right, on the **All Apps** screen. These   photos can also be accessed after installing a *file manager* app on the Nexus 7 or by connecting the Nexus 7 to another computer, as discussed on page 114. The photos can be found in the **Camera** folder, as follows:

Nexus 7>Internal Storage>DCIM>Camera

Taking Screenshots on the Nexus 7

You might want to show someone a copy of an interesting screen on the Nexus 7. Or you might want to include screenshots in some explanatory notes you are writing, such as this book. With the required screen displayed, simultaneously press the Power/Lock key (shown on page 12) and the Volume down key. You will hear the shutter noise and the screen shrinks and disappears. The screenshots are saved in the **Screenshot** folder in the **Gallery**, which can be accessed as described above. Alternatively using a file manager they can be found in:

Nexus 7>Internal Storage>Pictures>Screenshots

File Security
Viruses

These are small, malicious programs or apps designed to damage your files. Most, if not all of the apps you use on the Nexus 7 are installed from the Play Store. These have been checked for viruses before being accepted into the Play Store. Swipe down from the top right of the screen and select **SETTINGS** then **Security**. The settings below should prevent apps which may contain viruses from being installed.

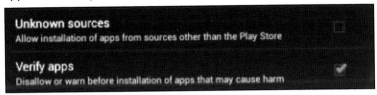

Making Backup Copies

If your only copies of files are in the clouds, you might delete one by mistake. As discussed on page 114, you could connect the Nexus 7 to a PC computer and copy files to a flash drive attached to the PC, by dragging and dropping or using Copy and Paste. Or install a *file manager* app on the Nexus 7.

Setting a Password on the Start Up Screen

You can set a password which must be entered on startup before the Nexus 7 can be used. Select **SETTINGS**, **Security** and **Screenlock**. Select **Password** and enter a suitable one. The following password entry bar will appear on the startup screen.

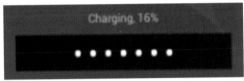

You can also set the screen lock to use **Slide** (or swipe), **Face Unlock** (facial recognition), a drawn **Pattern** or a **PIN** number.

Index

A

Aeroplane mode............49, 57
All Apps screen 26, 27, 28
Android O.S. 7
Apps 1, 7, 9, 25
    downloading, installing...38
    folders 30
    managing, deleting 39

B

Backup copies...................116
Battery............................11, 49
Bluetooth, pairing 22, 23
Bookmarks 83

C

Cameras................. 2, 26,115
Chrome browser ... 2, 9, 26,75
Cloud computing 2, 3
Cloud printing....................107

D

Downloading 74
Drive................................3, 16

E

eBooks 58-66
    deleting 65
E-mail............................16, 86
    attachment 88

F

Facebook 10, 30, 91
Favorites Tray 26
    customising 29
Files, security 116
Folders 30

G

Games 73
Gmail...............................9, 26
    account, Nexus 7 16
        PC or Mac.......16
Google
    Calendar 54-56
    Cards 42, 45
    Chrome 2, 9, 26, 75
    Docs.........................16, 99
        spreadsheet.........102
        word processing ..100
    Drive 3, 16, 97
    Earth 9
    Maps 26
    Now.................................42
    Play Books......................58
    Play Store 7, 9, 36, 60
    Search 9, 43
Google+ 96

H

Hangouts feature 26
History, browsing 84
Home Screens 25
    customizing....................31
    widgets.....................33-35

I

Importing files 110-112
Internal storage...................2

J

Jelly Bean O.S. 2

K

Keyboard
  Bluetooth 22
  On-screen 19
  USB 20
  wireless 21
Keyword search 78
Kindle 10
  App for Nexus 7 66

L

LinkedIn 95
Location access 48
Lock screen 12, 116

M

Magazines 67
Managing Nexus 7
  from a PC 114
Memory 2
Menu icon 18
Micro USB port 3, 11
Movies 70
Music 68
My Library 53, 59

N

Navigation bar 25
Nexus 7
  diagram 12
  starting up 12
NFC 23
Notifications 52

O

Opening PC files 113
Operating System 2
OTG cable 20

P

Password, Lock screen 116

Play Store 7, 9, 36, 60
Processor 2

Q

Quick Settings ... 15, 17, 22, 48

R

RAM 2

S

Screen resolution 2
Screen rotation 17, 49
Screenshots, taking 115
SD Cards 24, 110
Settings 13, 17, 47, 48, 50
Shutting down 17
Skype 5, 10, 30, 89
Solid State Drive 2
Speech/voice
  recognition 19, 24, 43
SSD (Solid State Drive) 2
Streaming 74
Stylus 4, 19
Syncing 56, 101, 103, 105

T

Tabbed browsing 81
Tablet computer, uses 5
Touchscreen 3
  gestures 18
TV, live, catchup 72
Twitter 10, 30, 93

U

USB hub 21

W

Web Address 77
Widgets 25, 27, 33
Wi-Fi, connecting 13-15, 48

Y

YouTube 10, 26, 71